MW00605076

Megan,

May you always follow your beautiful ♡!

Cheers to all that awaits you!

♡ Sarah

Sweetly Seeking

LIVING AN INSPIRED LIFE

Sweetly Seeking

LIVING AN INSPIRED LIFE

Published by

COOL CREATIVE PRESS
P.O. Box 238
Lisbon, OH 44432
www.coolcreativepress.com

Library of Congress Control Number: 2018955776

Publisher's Cataloging-In-Publication Data
(Prepared by The Donohue Group, Inc.)

Names: Dickey, Sarah L., author, photographer, compiler. | Aillery, Lorraine, writer of supplementary textual content.
Title: Sweetly seeking : living an inspired life / Sarah L. Dickey ; foreword by Lorraine Aillery.
Description: [Poland, Ohio] : [Cool Creative Press], [2019] | "A compilation of inspirational pieces by Sarah L. Dickey and other writers."
Identifiers: ISBN 9780999072011
Subjects: LCSH: Spiritual life--Quotations, maxims, etc. | Spiritual life--Pictorial works.
Classification: LCC PS3604.I35 S94 2019 | DDC 811/.6--dc23

Editor: Gail M. Kearns, www.topressandbeyond.com
Copy editor: Joni Wilson
Book and cover design: The Book Designers
Book production coordinated by To Press & Beyond
Cool Creative Press logo designed by Starr Struck Studio
Images courtesy of the author

Printed in Canada

To all of the beautiful souls who have inspired me to sweetly seek. Thank you for being my teachers and for instilling a curiosity deep within my soul to live a life marked with love, adventure, and grace.

FOREWORD

It seemed unremarkable and prosaic at the time, but, in looking back, it was a turning point in a decisive moment.

In a spontaneous and unrehearsed act, I cut down a rather large and withered bush on a neglected piece of ground. Located in a courtyard that is bound by sidewalks and a stairwell, I knew that this spot was an odd place to plant a flower garden. But I was willing to give it a try.

At first, I cleared the debris and prepared the soil, while at times I chuckled at the absurdity of this venture. My resolve was frequently challenged by the overload of strain on my body. Yet, my heart, undaunted, never doubted. I was perplexed by the spirited drive that stimulated my commitment to this project.

For the next six years, neighbors and passersby were bemused and curious. They watched as I worked endless hours in the glaring sun and long after nightfall.

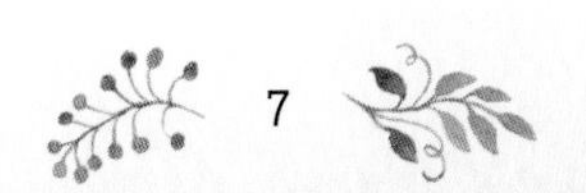

My mistakes and setbacks were evident but they taught me well. I became intimate with the complexity of how sunlight, soil, water, and the personalities of plants interact with each sector of the garden.

Eventually, from this forsaken piece of dirt emerged a resplendent exhibition of color and form. The scilla and astilbe, trollius and columbine, cosmos and anemone flowers are all a community, deeply rooted and energized in the soul of their place.

Creating a work of art begins in the heart. The ultimate canvas is our life. In our imagination, boundaries are nonexistent, risks are possibilities, and fear is motivation. Inspired action can be cloaked in the commonplace. A daily endeavor is elevated to ritual.

This garden transformed me.

Words can provide the promise of a gateway when seeded within our own inner landscape.

Sarah Dickey's visionary parlance is like a pathway. Sarah is impelled to walk into the heart of the mystery. She graciously wanders in a rich and nuanced world, at times with some hesitation, but always with an optimist's certainty of discovering the treasure.

She wrestles with contradiction—"Ushering in a space of not knowing welcomes a universal kind of magic."

Then she opens her heart to the headwinds—"Learn to sit in the midst of the storm."

And finally, Sarah arrives at her treasure—"Reflect your brilliance into a thousand drops of water" where "Life has been constructing a masterpiece through you."

Her book, *Sweetly Seeking: Living an Inspired Life,* is an invitation to a glimpse into the spiritual garden where Sarah "lives the questions" on the path to her own awakening.

Lorraine Aillery
Boulder, Colorado

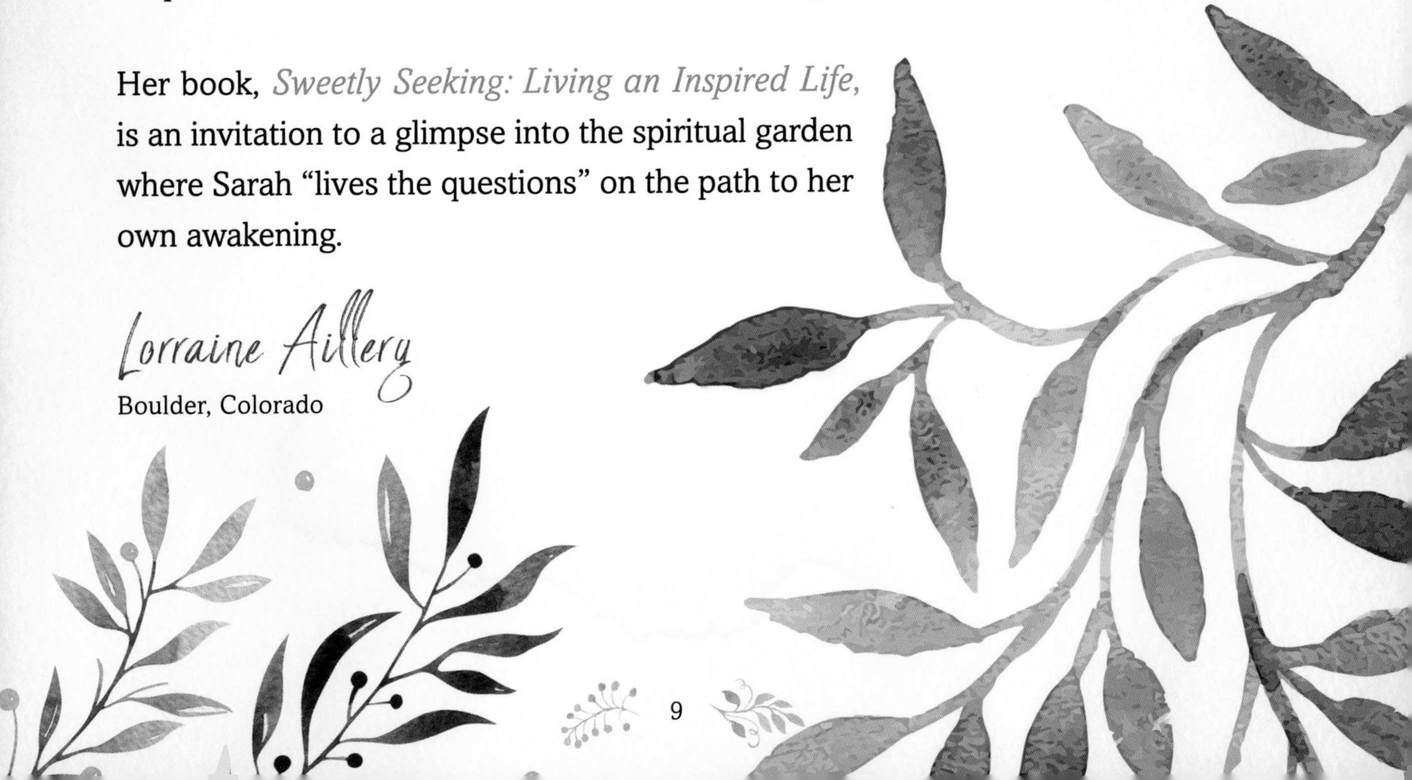

INTRODUCTION

My dear friend, Lorraine, offers such classic wisdom about the ultimate cultivation of one's truest desires. It is my belief that we are all "planting the spiritual gardens of our hearts." We are continually invited to unearth the treasures of our lives. To seek with zeal and amazement that which lies hidden and that which lies in plain sight.

There is the proverbial season of preparation in which we begin to nourish the various territories of our hearts. We clear out the old so that we might truly usher in new growth.

It is in this planting that we begin to seek and discover the magic of our craft. Perhaps we spend years in the same regions of awareness, nourishing ourselves so that we might truly appreciate the bounty that awaits us. When we present the universe with our willing hearts we can expect miracles to unfold.

The journey of sweetly seeking is the journey of a lifetime. There is no sense of arrival, rather a continual refinement of one's life. Life wildly calls out to us. It is up to us to exclaim, "Yes. Yes, I am ready even if my knees are shaking and my heart is racing. Yes, I am ready to sweetly seek."

We prepare for the unfoldment of the sacred breezes. We accept the invitations to grow and change. We honor the times of transition and hibernation. We highlight the glorious rays of the sun that re-enliven our spirits. It is in this spiritual garden that we weather the storms and gracefully accept the seasons of our lives.

For as long as I can remember, I have been seeking life in the most curious of ways. I have ventured down unmarked alleys. I have also stayed in situations, over-riding my inner knowing. I have succumbed to fears, and I have also taken flight. Life continually orchestrates greater ways of being. Surrender is possible. Peace is available. Love is infinitely present.

Life is constantly offering me the exact medicine I need to grow and evolve. Do you know this to be true in your life also?

"The universe buries strange jewels deep within us all, and then stands back to see if we can find them."
-Elizabeth Gilbert

It is my hope that these passages inspire you on your journey. Perhaps they will become like an old friend, or maybe they will allow you to sit in a space of compassion, or just maybe you will open to a page and not feel so alone.

However these passages resonate with you, I hope they offer you the encouragement to sweetly seek in the spiritual garden of your heart. Take flight, my friends!

All my love,

Sarah

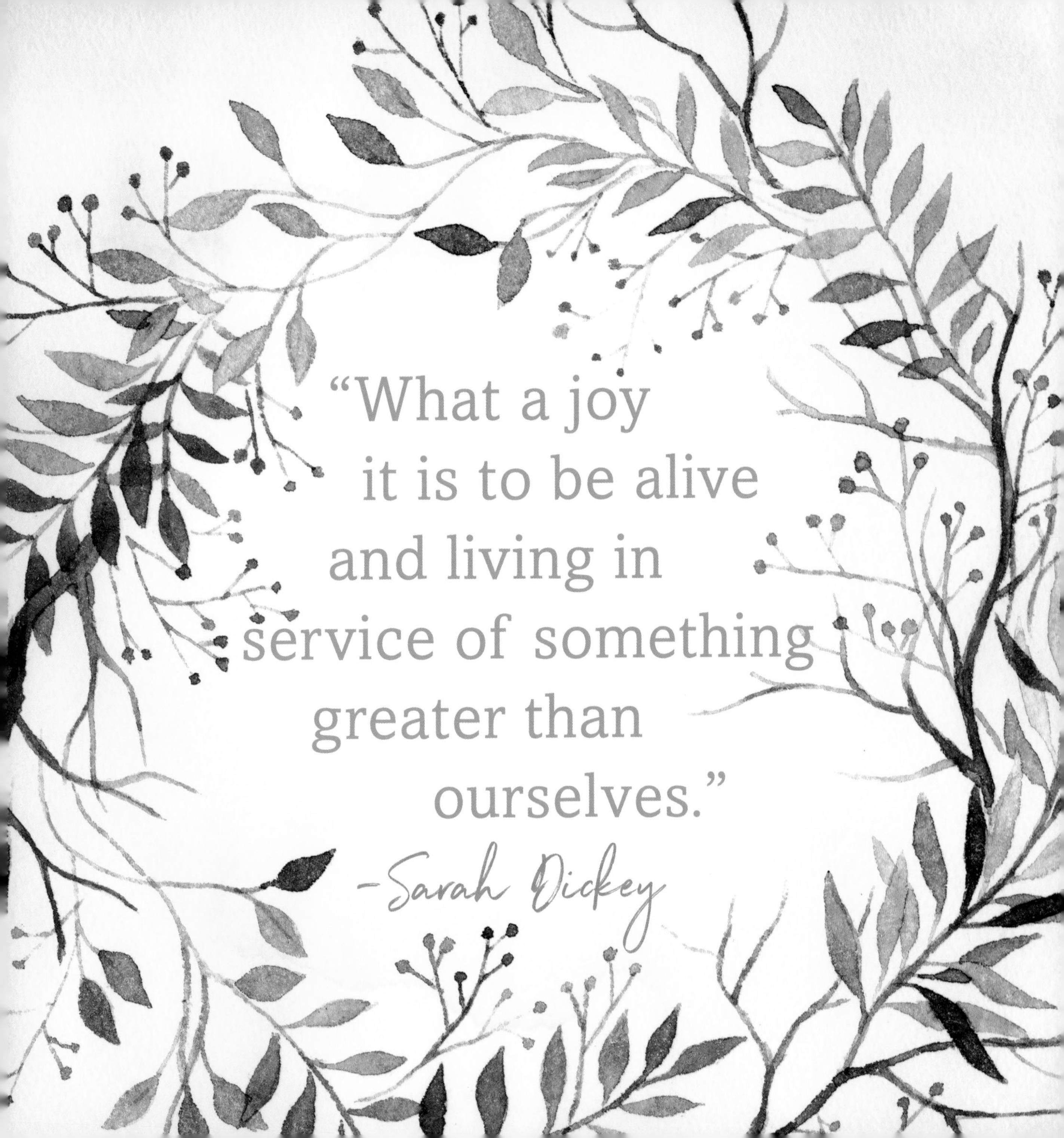
"What a joy
it is to be alive
and living in
service of something
greater than
ourselves."
-Sarah Dickey

Ecstasy

Let life take your breath away . . .
Soften into the unknown and cultivate
a willingness to thrive in your life.
Manifest miracles.
Delight in relationships.
Honor the journey.
Return time and time again.
You are a sacred part of the unfolding.
A divine expression of the grandest love.
Share your authentic light.

"I have a deeply hidden and inarticulate desire for something beyond the daily life."

-Virginia Woolf

Tiny Human

Your heart so tenderly traverses around mine.

Boundless in depth.

Limitless in size.

I memorize these moments.

I tuck them in the corridors of my heart.

Laughter radiates, warmth grows my adoration.

You are divine just as you are.

Full of wonder.

Decorated in love.

Brimming with possibilities.

Unfold your own dreams.

Live with childlike wonder . . . all the days of your life.

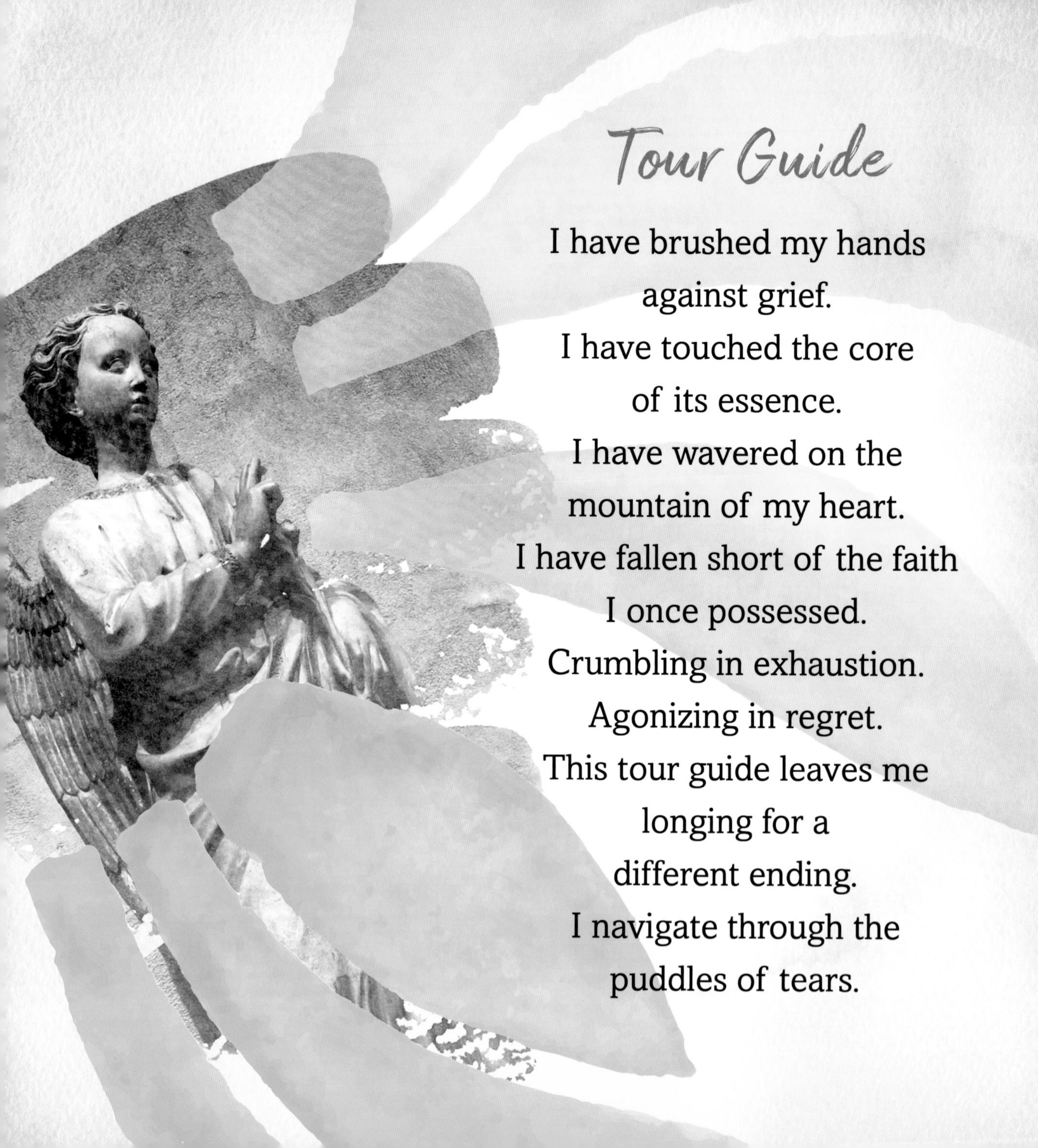

Tour Guide

I have brushed my hands
against grief.
I have touched the core
of its essence.
I have wavered on the
mountain of my heart.
I have fallen short of the faith
I once possessed.
Crumbling in exhaustion.
Agonizing in regret.
This tour guide leaves me
longing for a
different ending.
I navigate through the
puddles of tears.

I touch my heart.
I close my eyes and stumble
into its entirety.
This ache is also my
grandest desire.
I inquire again of this
tour guide,
"Can you love your grief as
you have loved love?
These two friends are
entwined in a lifelong tender
embrace."
Seek to know them within
the walls of your own
country.

"Sorrow prepares you
for joy. It violently
sweeps everything out
of your house, so that
new joy can find space
to enter."

-Rumi

Courage

Dear Life,

I am not so sure what you expect of me, but I can tell you that I have gathered my gratitude and hope to again come to the edge of life. I want to dance in the rays of the lemony sun. I long to love again. Really love. Wildly love. Passionately love. To place my heart against the heartbeat of the earth. To place my hand upon my lover's face and linger in the in-between. To touch my own heart and feel courage rising like a satisfied river. I'm ready, life. Swallow me, so that I might swim again.

All my love.

Yes

One of the most amazing lessons we have garnered along the way has been to see every instance as a courageous invitation to live from our hearts. Allow that space to be messy, complex, sophisticated, simple . . . whatever it needs to be so that we say, "Yes!" Pair your "yes" moments with gratitude and watch your life become a springboard of possibilities. Touch your "yes" moments and anchor them into every instance of your life.

"There are only two ways to live your life. One is as though nothing is a miracle. The other is as though everything is a miracle."

-Albert Einstein

Surrender

I soften into the earth and feel the support of life humming below the surface. I soften my thoughts. I dissolve my desires and explore the notion of simply letting go. Each muscle in my body surrenders to the ground. I wonder how my entire life could be embodied in this posture. How would life flow more intentionally? This pose allows me to settle in and feel the happenings of life. So tiresome to hold on.

So freeing to let go.

Artist

Do not paint what you see or sculpt what
you can hold. Craft a life that dispels
the ordinary. Run wild through the halls
of your heart. Fashion a life dripping
with authenticity. Allow your craft, your
profession, your life to be extraordinary.
What? Express the deepest spaces of your
being so that you can take a full breath.
Agree to living a creative life. Transform any
beliefs that keep you from coloring outside
the lines. Splash. Sing. Capture. Offer.
Make this tapestry of art your life.

“It is better to live your own destiny imperfectly than to life an imitation of somebody else’s life with perfection.”

–Bhagavad Gita

Creating

Ushering in a space of not knowing
welcomes a universal kind of magic.
Be soft. Be strong.
Be willing to be amazed.
Hold a space for your deepest
desires to unfold. Match your
energy with the desires
in your heart.
Fashion a life that is overflowing
with marvelous magic.

New Year

Allow your possibilities to be as
infinite as the field before you.
Invite success into your life.
Claim your joys.
Love your tribe and yourself.
Say yes to adventure.
Say no to energy drainers.
Honor the spaces between.
Connect to your divine nature.
Master intention setting.
Cultivate a new year again and again.
Day after day.
Year after year.

"We don't see things as they are; we see them as we are."

-Anaïs Nin

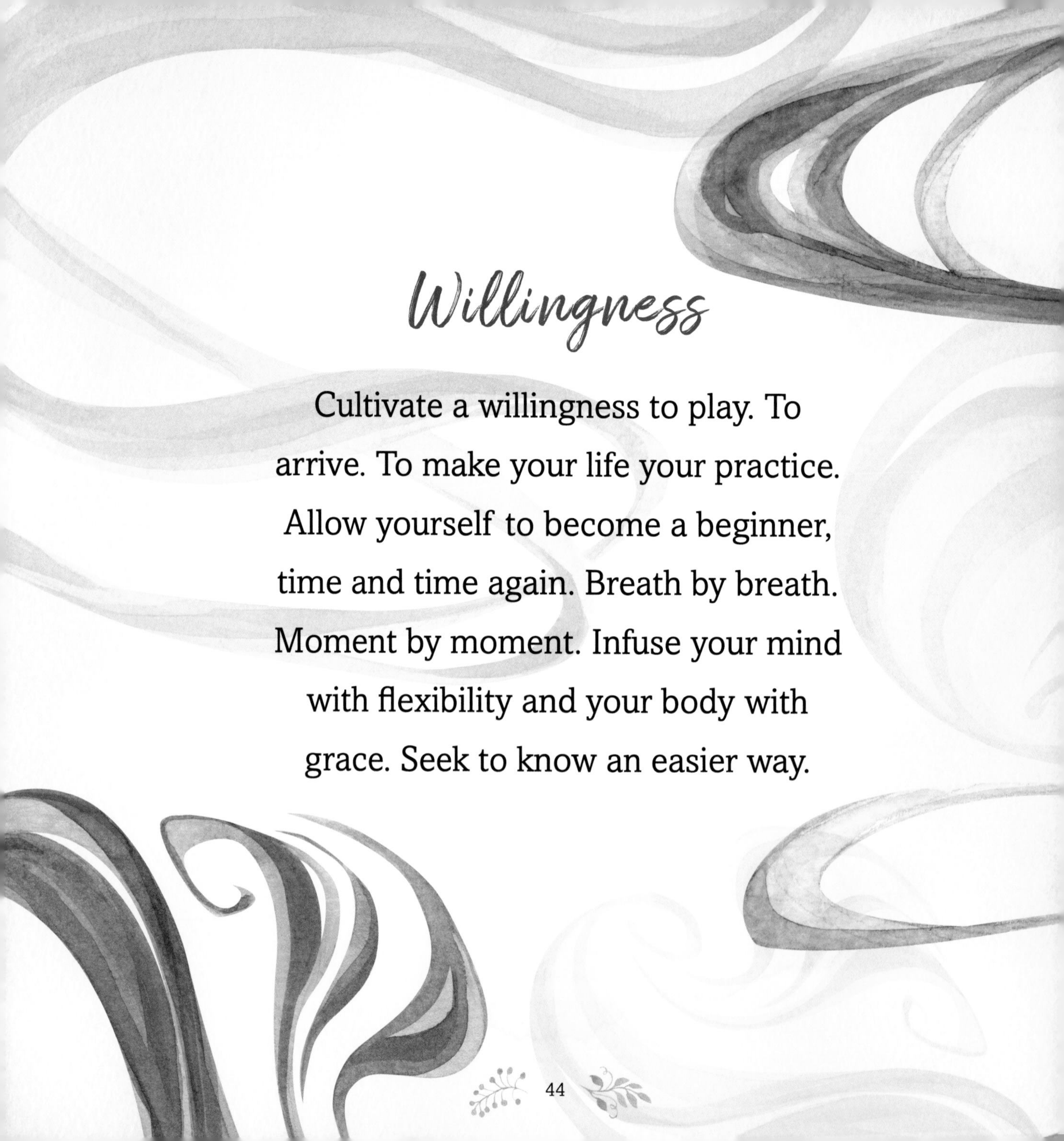

Willingness

Cultivate a willingness to play. To arrive. To make your life your practice. Allow yourself to become a beginner, time and time again. Breath by breath. Moment by moment. Infuse your mind with flexibility and your body with grace. Seek to know an easier way.

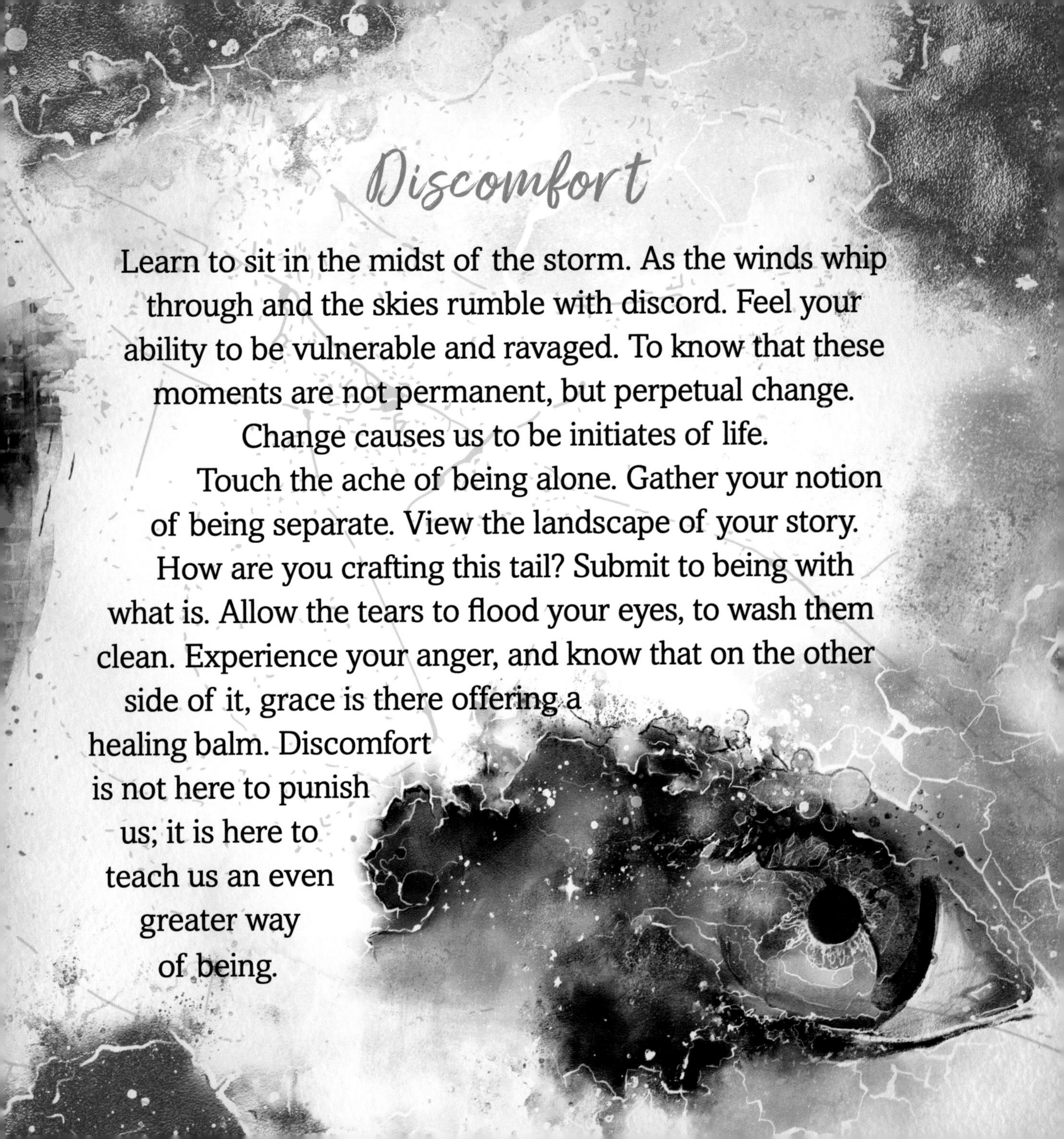

Discomfort

Learn to sit in the midst of the storm. As the winds whip through and the skies rumble with discord. Feel your ability to be vulnerable and ravaged. To know that these moments are not permanent, but perpetual change. Change causes us to be initiates of life.

Touch the ache of being alone. Gather your notion of being separate. View the landscape of your story. How are you crafting this tail? Submit to being with what is. Allow the tears to flood your eyes, to wash them clean. Experience your anger, and know that on the other side of it, grace is there offering a healing balm. Discomfort is not here to punish us; it is here to teach us an even greater way of being.

"When we are no
longer able to change
a situation … we are
challenged to change
ourselves."

-Victor E. Frankl

Freefall

Dissolve into the newness of this moment.
Drop the chains of whom you used to be.
Surrender into the plunge.
Feel the magnitude of blessings dancing with you.
Soak in the glory rays of divine love.
You are an exquisite being.
Rely on divine timing.
Elevate your vantage point.
Nourish your ability to cultivate resiliency.
Close your eyes.
Place your hand on your heart.
Swear your unique magic to life.
Fly free.
Jump.

Magic

Laugh.
Create.
Keep dreaming.
Fiercely follow your heart.
Awaken to the moment.
Have the courage and willingness to share your gifts and
watch them inspire the world.
Discover what makes your heart sing.
Embrace the edges of your discomfort.
Notice the possibilities on the other side of this distress.
Shift your story.
Take a deep breath.
Do your personal healing work.
See . . . see the beautiful people and views all around you.
Return to nature.
Be open to new adventures.
You never know what magic is coming to you!

“The privilege of
a lifetime is being
who you are.”

-Joseph Campbell

Verde

What a joy it is to be alive!
To live under the canopy of green.
To love amid the dazzling light!
To breathe in the many possibilities!
Flood your life with gratitude!
Believe that life is abundant and rich with color.

Light

Shine your light.

Cultivate a prosperous life.

Be intentional.

Clear away old energies.

Radiate from the center of your being.

Share the sparks of your spirit.

Kindle the light and

blaze forth.

“To live is the rarest
thing in the world.
Most people exist,
that is all.”

-Oscar Wilde

Fly

Fly higher.

Dream bigger.

Take a deep breath.

Discern when to stay and when to go.

No regrets as you soar.

Higher and higher.

Lighter.

Freer.

This is how you were meant to see the world.

Reflection

Awake to this moment.

Allow it to touch your heart.

Say, "Yes."

Breathe in the excitement.

Prepare.

Allow this moment to crack open your fearless heart.

Reflect your brilliance into a thousand drops of water.

Magnificent.

Timeless.

Reflection.

Why not you?

Why not me?

Why not now?

“With everything that has happened to you, you can either feel sorry for yourself or treat what has happened as a gift. Everything is either an opportunity to grow or an obstacle to keep you from growing. You get to choose.”

–Wayne W. Dyer

ZOOLIGHTS
Nov 27–
WILDLIGHTS
E THE ZOO
RIGHTER
THAN EVER
HANDLE
WITH CARE
CHRISTMAS
CAROL
Nov 27–Dec 30
Who's
Afraid
of
Dec 3–20
This
Christmas
DO IT ANYWAY
DEAD RE?
VOXX
XX ROMANA
Relax-n-unwind

Keep creating and refining the vision of your life!

Trust your beautiful, wild, creative, authentic light.

Share this unique light with the world.

Show up time and time again.

Say, “Yes.”

Repeat.

Touched

Every time we are touched by the
kindness of the universe,
We are reminded to
be kind to self and others.
The wellspring of love that animates
our lives is eternal.
Allow your soft heart to
be caressed by love.

“There is nothing more truly artistic than to love people.”

-Vincent van Gogh

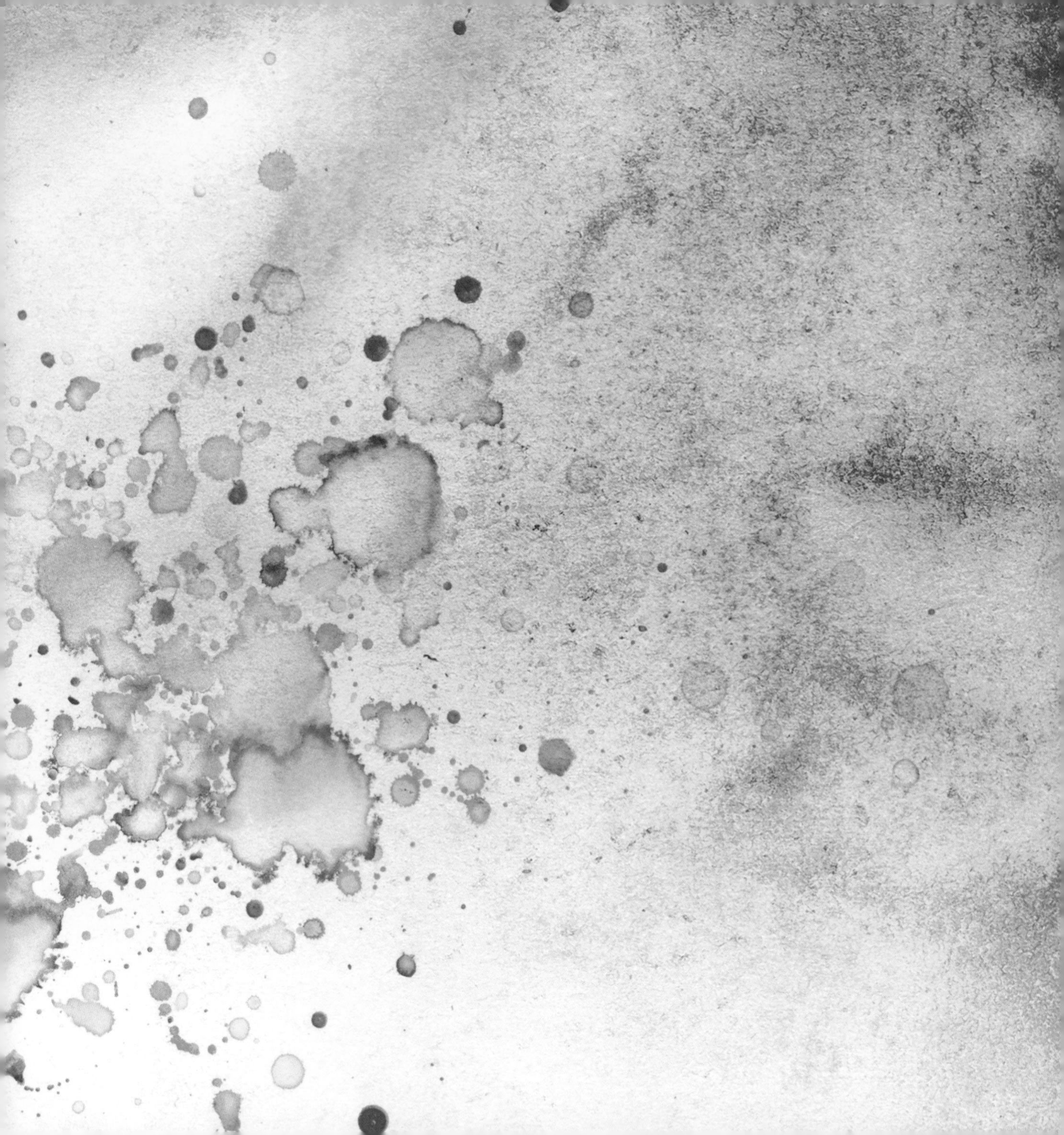

Be . . .

Be limitless.
Be beautiful.
Be a knockout.
Be wise.
Be kind.
Be intuitive.
Be fierce.
Be soft.
Be healthy.
Be sacred.
Be wonder.
Be joy.
No excuses.
No apologies.
No regrets.
Be you.

"What if I fall?
Oh, but my
darling, what if
you fly?"

-Erin Hanson

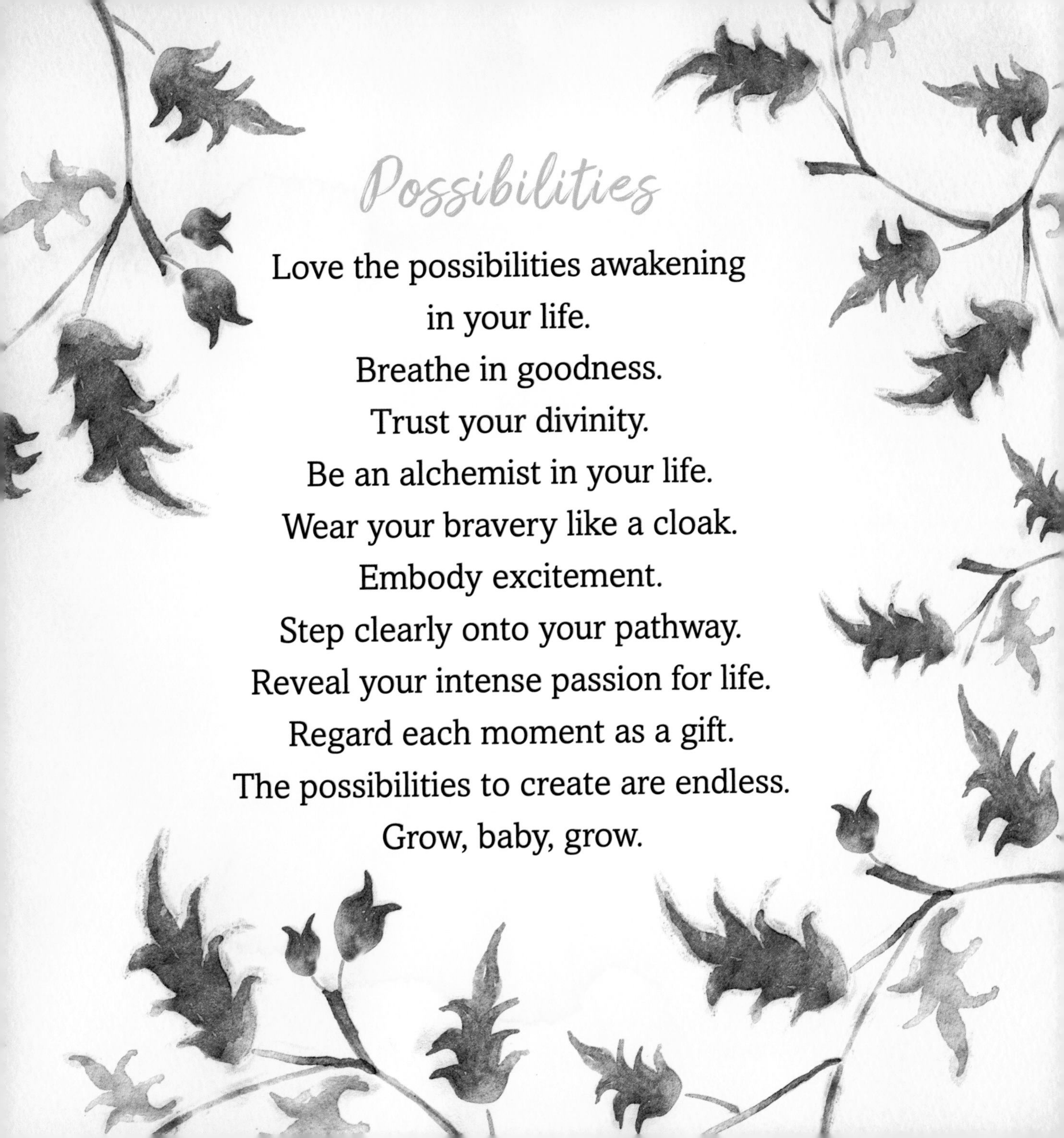

Possibilities

Love the possibilities awakening
in your life.
Breathe in goodness.
Trust your divinity.
Be an alchemist in your life.
Wear your bravery like a cloak.
Embody excitement.
Step clearly onto your pathway.
Reveal your intense passion for life.
Regard each moment as a gift.
The possibilities to create are endless.
Grow, baby, grow.

Adventure

Slide down the hill of wonder.

Jump off the cliff of desire.

Commit to new experiences.

Cultivate a willingness to touch the rhythm of your journey.

Lay on the earth and feel your heart beat.

Swim in the ocean of possibility.

Behold the magnificence of a sunrise.

Dream with the moon, as it tucks its heart into the velvet sky.

What path is calling your name?

Trust the grandest adventure . . . your life!

Share

Our gorgeous hearts are alive and well in every instance.
Share your beauty.
Unfold into your vulnerability.
Radiate light.
Behold your magnificence.
Sit with the questions.
Transform your sufferings.
Share your heart with the world.
Share your novel voice.
Share your tender touch.
Share all of yourself as you stand
in the glory of your
beingness.

We are all becoming.
Each moment of our lives is calling us to be an updated
version of ourselves.
Laboring through the birth of becoming.
Perhaps we have had an easy way.
Or maybe we have struggled through
the narrow openings of life.
At our core, we are magnificent in our essence.
We are radiant beings of infinite light.
We weather storms.
We persevere.
We flourish.
We bloom.
We become.

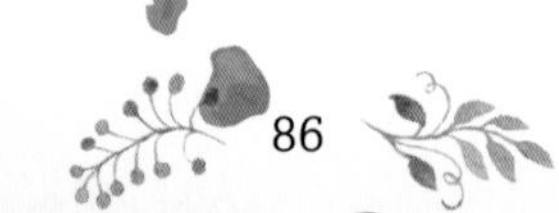

Blue skies.

Green grass.

Feeling the vibe of Mother Earth.

Making my way into a shape of openness.

Coming to an edge and loving the process.

Feeling transformed.

Resting in opportunity.

Growing into new possibilities.

"Life isn't about finding yourself. Life is about creating yourself."

-George Bernard Shaw

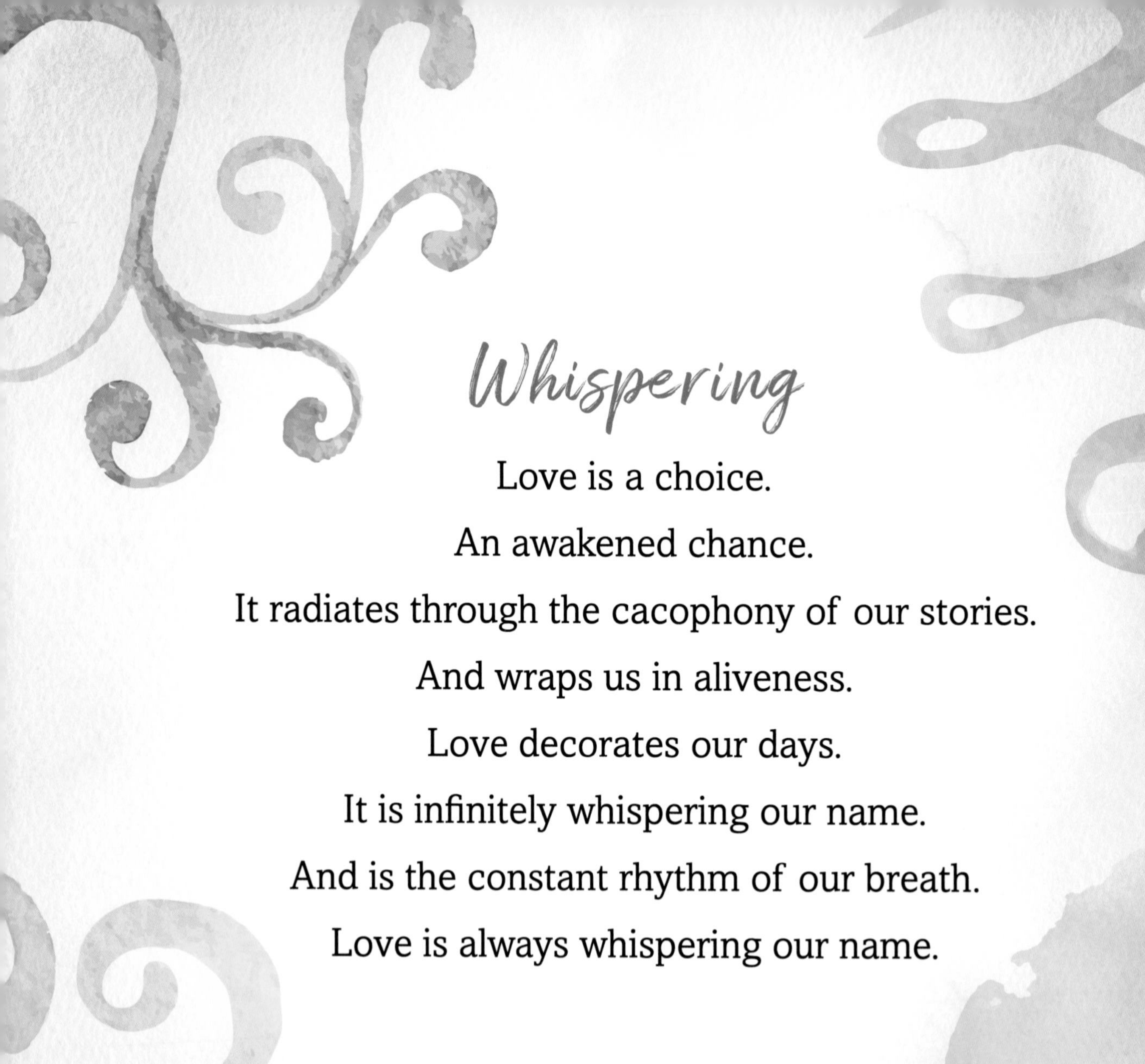

Whispering

Love is a choice.

An awakened chance.

It radiates through the cacophony of our stories.

And wraps us in aliveness.

Love decorates our days.

It is infinitely whispering our name.

And is the constant rhythm of our breath.

Love is always whispering our name.

"The heart is a
Thousand-stringed
instrument
That can only be tuned
with love."

-Hafiz

Upside Down

Practice.

Practice.

Practice.

Flush your fears!

Change your perspective!

Go upside downside.

Be willing to be a beginner.

Align with your intentions.

Animate your actions.

Continually align and refine.

Last Leaf

Be willing to be the last one.

Sit with your discomfort.

Sit with your joy.

Embody your truth.

Your life is your message.

How do you show up when no one else remains?

Who are you at your core?

Cultivate a willingness to be suspended until divine timing moves you.

Live inspired.

Trust the wait.

“In three words I can sum up everything I’ve learned about life: it goes on.”

-Robert Frost

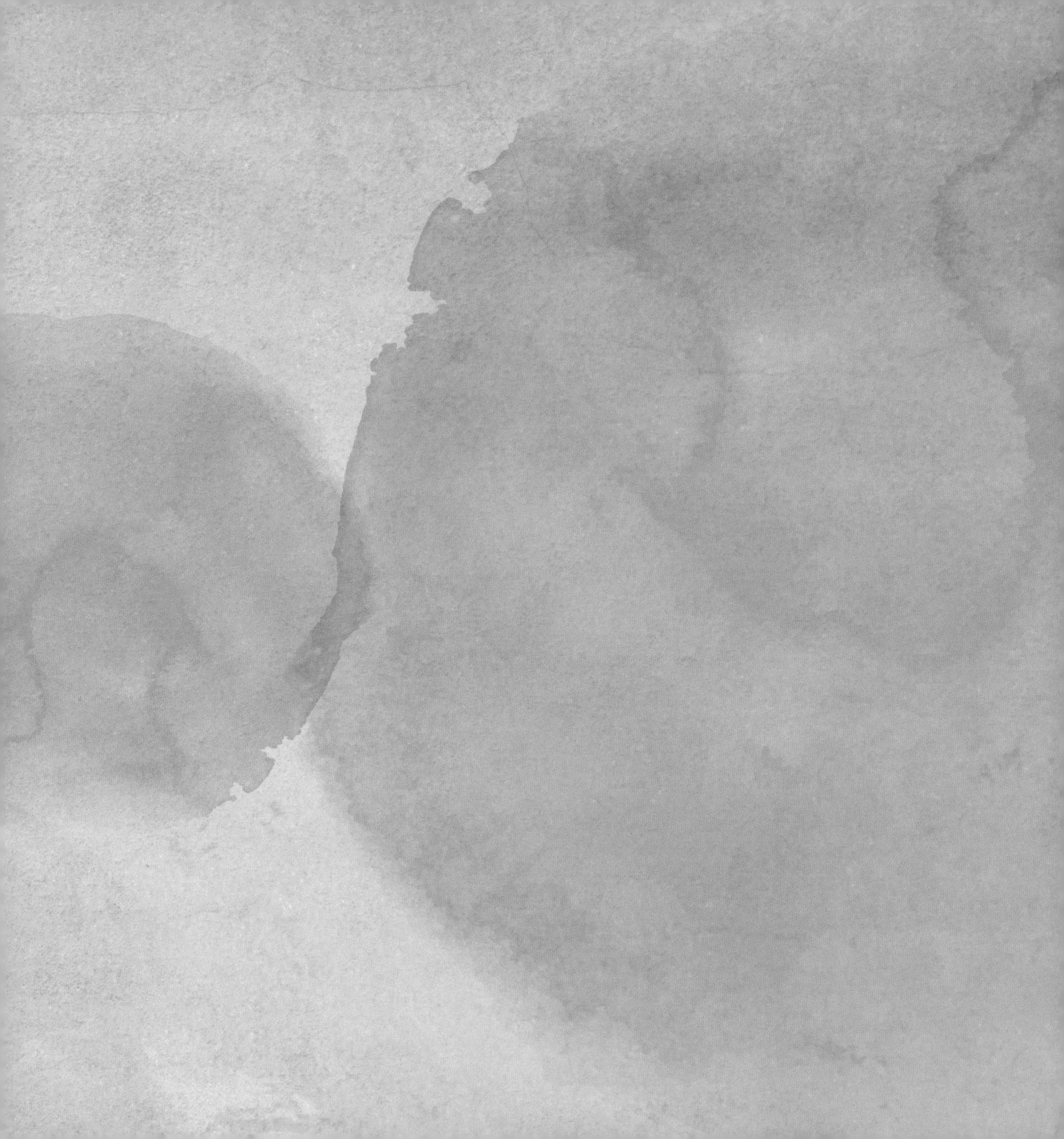

Cement Heart

Right there . . .
That spot you were about to step on.
That's love saying, "I'm here."
Love asks us to notice its simplicity and its majesty.
Love is soft.
Love is solid.
Love is the current of unraveling.
Love is the sweet surrender of our tears.
Love is our sanctuary.
Love is our classroom.
Love is always in plain sight, in the simpleness of living.
Pause in this moment.
How is love surrounding you?
How are you surrounding love?

Traversing

I continue to traverse this desert of anticipation
Tracing the outlines of excitement
Stumbling on the hills of promise.
Living into the shapes of the landscape.
I traverse like a wild woman.
Sure of all that is to come.
Open to all that has yet to be discovered.

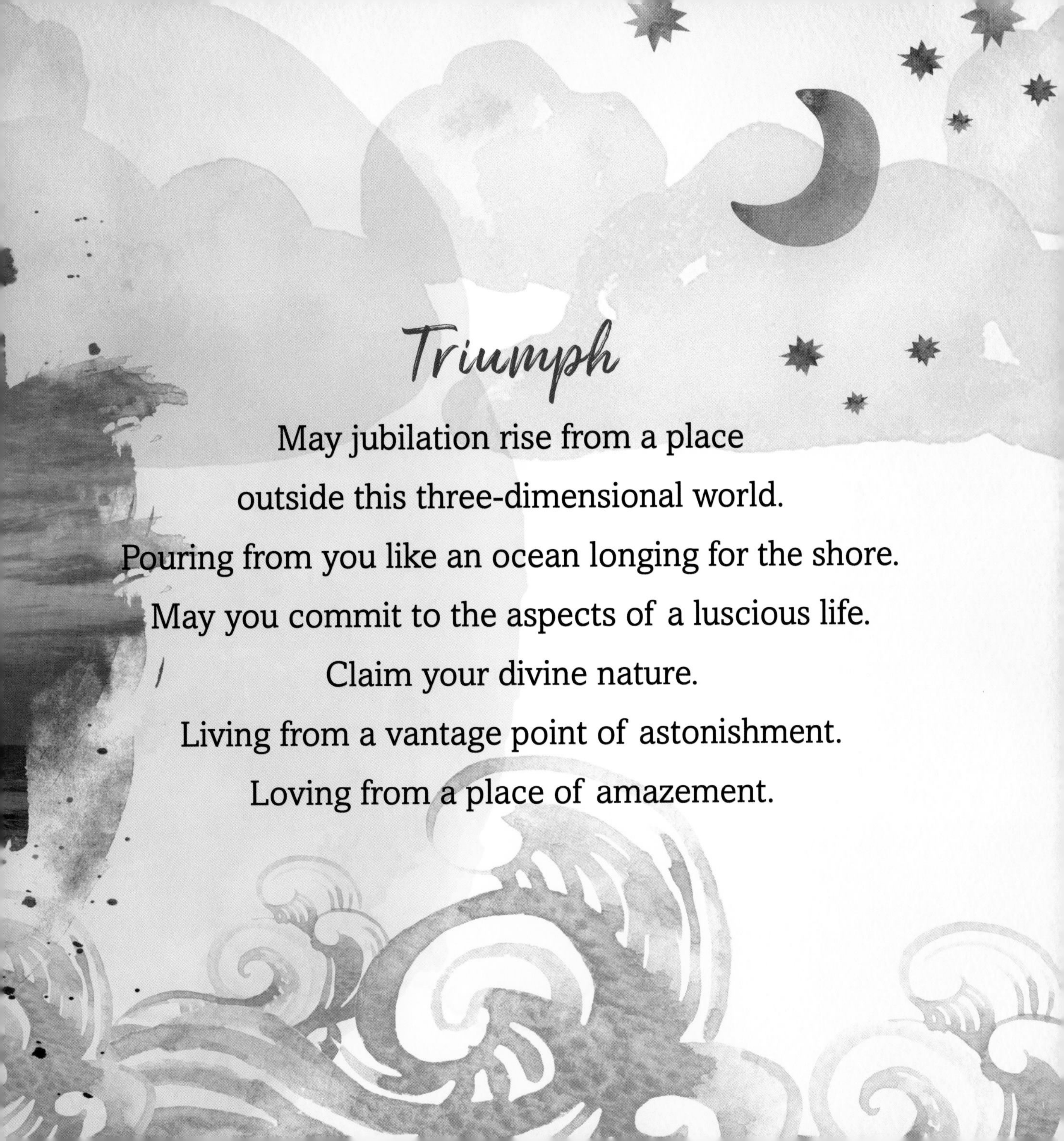

Triumph

May jubilation rise from a place
outside this three-dimensional world.
Pouring from you like an ocean longing for the shore.
May you commit to the aspects of a luscious life.
Claim your divine nature.
Living from a vantage point of astonishment.
Loving from a place of amazement.

"Those who don't believe in magic will never find it."

-Roald Dahl

Overflowing

Allow your life to overflow with goodness.

Awaken to the abundance of the earth.

Look up into the glory of the sky.

Expand in all four directions.

Be consumed with the ebb and flow.

Meet yourself on the banks of life's river.

Drenched with prosperity.

Overflow with blessings.

Savasana

Allow the earth to become a platform of surrender.

Melt into every ache that lingers in your heart.

Circulate your breath into the life in-between

Abandon the longing.

Relinquish your grasp.

Soften your face.

Lessen your attachments.

Feel your brilliance.

Be transformed.

Let go, body.

Let go, breath.

Let go, mind.

Savasana.

“Be still and know that I am God.”

-Psalm 46

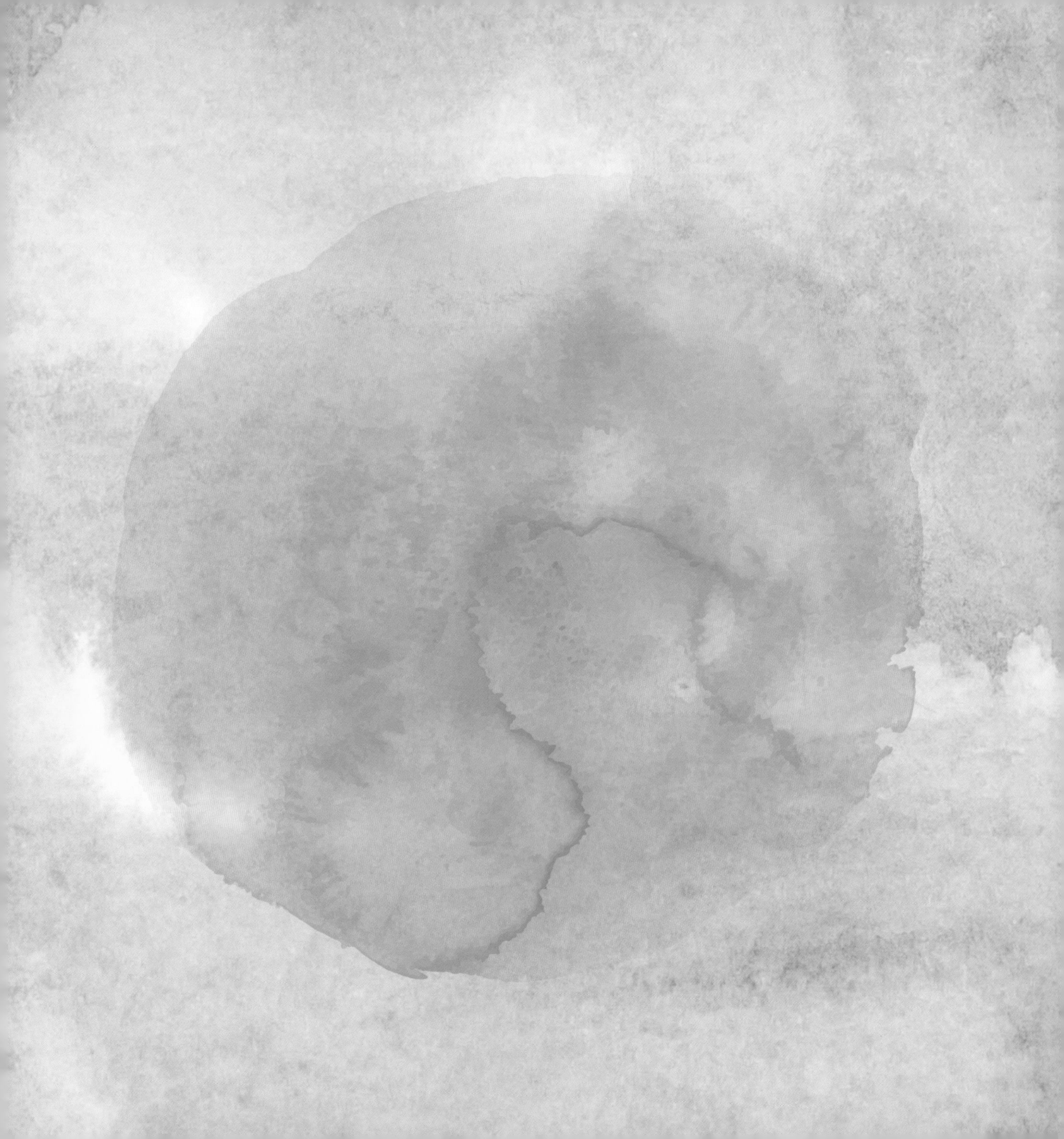

Chakras

Illuminate your crown to
absolute connectivity.
You, darling light, are radiant
with possibility.
See clearly all that lies before you.
Confident in your knowing,
Speak your life into existence.
Impart the truths of your journey.
Land in the center of your being . . .
Sit in the plentiful field of your heart.
Touch the sorrow.
Honor the luxurious
offerings from love.
Know that the complexities of life
are also classrooms of love.
Give thanks for the way that life has
tended to your unique soul.
Journey into your unique power.
Radiate with conviction
and purpose.
Offer your light to the world, as sure
as the rays of the sun.
Voyage into the belly of
your passions.
Offer this space so that
you can become
pregnant with opportunities,
Sensual and free.
Express the wildness of creativity
that animates your world.
Dive into the foundation of
your existence.
Stand firm, rooted in the
truths of your heart,
Grounded in the philosophy
of your soul,
Open to the evolution of your
incomparable journey.

"You have to grow from the inside out. None can teach you, none can make you spiritual. There is no other teacher but your own soul."

–Swami Vivekananda

63

Asmita

I often cling to who I think I am.
I am a woman full of desire.
My belly overflowing with possibilities.
My life flanked with inspiration.
My heart reaching for love.
My hands aching to create.
I reach to the stars, daring to become nothing,
Seeking to become everything.
Life keeps whispering, "Let go of whom you think you are."
Become dazzled with the likelihood that this will be
a practice for the entirety of my life.
Let go of titles.
Let go of possessions.
Let go of judgments.
If I am not these things, then who am I?
Who am I?
Maybe these titles are an illusion.
Help me to wake.
Help me to remember,
I am . . .

Here Are the Messengers That Bring Sweet Peace

Sitting between worlds, I watch you with such intrigue.
Studying the decay of your physical form.
Seeing your spiritual body grow stronger.
Conversations from the ethers
Whisper from your past.
I wonder about all the worlds you see.
I wonder how long this will last.
Your mumblings seem to offer comfort.
Your transmissions grant me a certain peace.
Who are these messengers that are
bringing you sweet peace?

"The question is not what you look at, but what you see."

-Henry David Thoreau

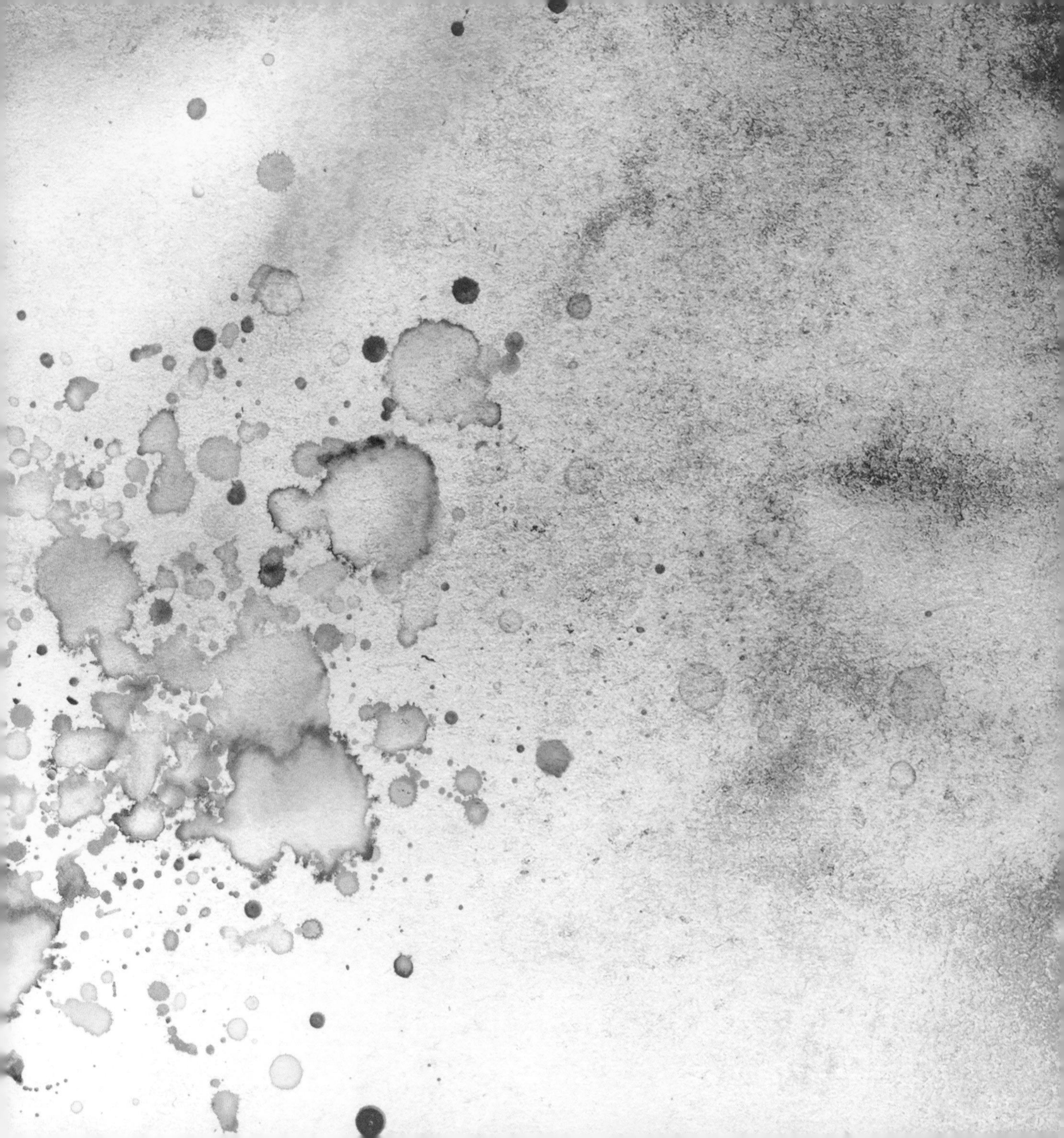

Touching

As we touch our own hearts,
We greatly expand our capacity to
be love and to show love.
When I can sit in the center of joy,
I realize that I can express joy.
When I sit in the midst of my sorrow,
I realize I can also express sorrow.
Happiness, joy, sorrow, love.
All these wondrous, transformative emotions
Here for me to experience and express.
Present in my midst so that I might transform.
Offering me teachings so that I might grow.
Dissolve into gratitude.
Clinging to nothingness.
Life touches my heart time and time again.

Belief

What good is knowledge if we profess to know everything?
What benefit is devotion if we attach an outcome?
What edges do we miss if we stay on the sidelines of life?
What adventures do we say no to because we are afraid?
What dreams do we squash because we think we aren't ready?
What love do we squander because we haven't
forgiven ourselves?
What do we practice day in and day out?
What if we sat in the center of our hearts and declared
to live our lives in amazement?
Believing that all is possible.
Feeling free in our practices of living.
Knowing that noble ways of being are awaiting us.
Believe.

Mirror

When was the last time you gazed into your own eyes?
Can you muster compassion for this image staring back at you?
Dissolving into the stories of your life,
Can you hold a tender fragment of kindness for your journey thus far?
All the benevolent sentiments that you share with others,
Can you absorb them into your center?
The lines that decorate your face,
Can you fully inhabit their origins?
The grief that snatched your joy.
The love that pieced you back together.
The ebb and flow of life on the delicate tracings of your face.
You are beautiful.
Can you fathom that?
Life has been constructing a masterpiece through you.
Authentically unique.
Deliciously beautiful.
Savor this moment of seeing.
Allow life to reflect.
See with gentleness all that life has offered you.

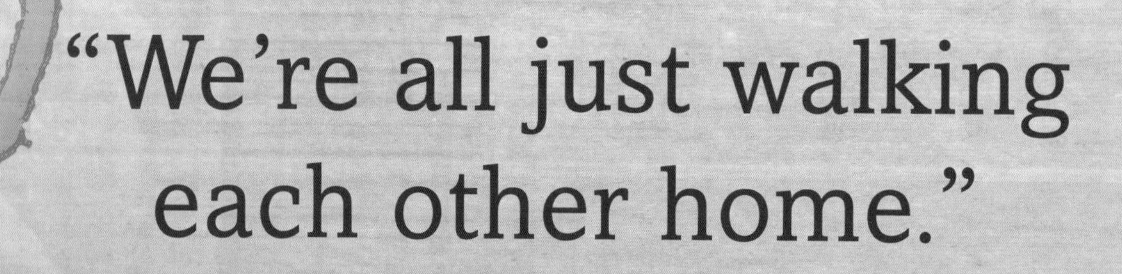

-Ram Dass

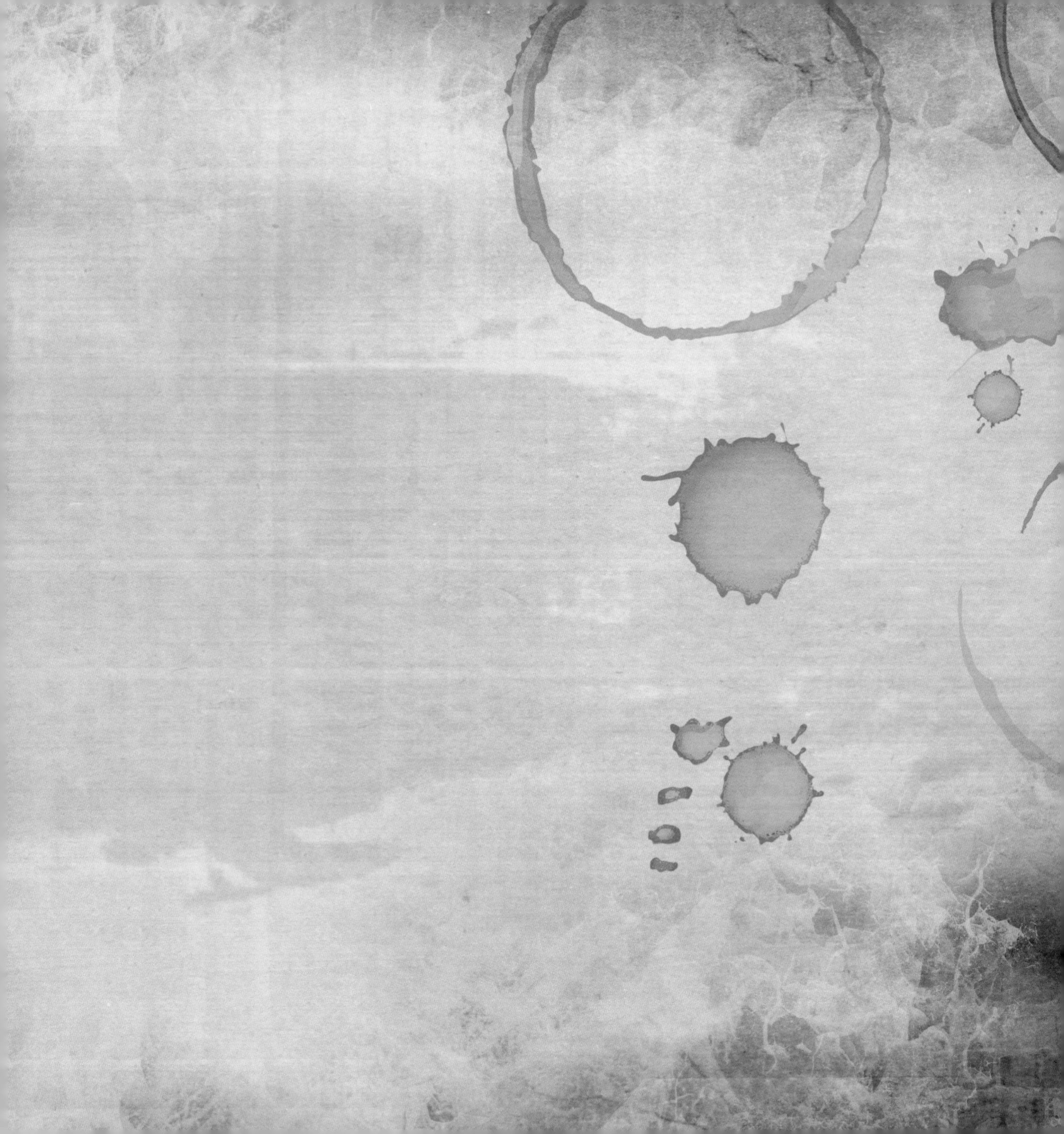

Travel

Be willing to fly into the unknown,
Exploring the wilderness,
Touching down in the foreign lands of your heart.
Tending to the wild paths of potentials,
Gather adventures into your being.
Stockpile them onto the map of your heart.
Get lost in not knowing.
Wake among the stars.
Feeling your soul dazzled with radiant light,
Grow amid the rays of the sun.
Cultivating an attitude of thriving in your life,
Travel with new eyes.
Climb the mountains that take your breath away.
Lie among the shores.
Dream in the fields of opportunities.
Swim in the still waters.
Get lost in the unknown,
Time and time again . . .

Show Up

Show up for your physical body so that
you can show up for your life.
Each day create movement toward your goals.
Be kind in your thoughts.
Be curious about your edges.
Become a warrior of intentional effort.
Curious about the edges of your physical body.
Serious about moving from a wellspring of joy.
What if every movement originated
from the center of loving thought?
Grow your strength.
Increase your capacity.
Cultivate kindness.
Resolve to love yourself!
Show up.
Time and time again.

"You yourself, as much as anybody in the entire universe, deserve your love and affection."

-Sharon Salzberg

Do What
You Love

Themes

The universe is always weaving
themes together in our lives.
See them.
Feel them.
Hear them.
The body is the temple for our souls.
Nourish it.
Honor it.
Simplify it.
Allow yourself to be curious
About how life is moving through
The vessel of you.
Honor the theme in this season of your life.

“There are years that ask questions and years that answer.”

-Zora Neale Hurston

Beauty

Be your own kind of beautiful.
Walk humbly.
Smile often.
Seek to share love.
Know yourself.
Cultivate kindness.
Wish on stars.
Cuddle with puppies.
Sing in the shower.
Sip on coffee in bed.
Linger with your lover.
Cultivate gratitude.
Jump in puddles.
Look up often.
Pause in the midst of wonder.
Know that you are a living, breathing wonder.
Radiate good vibes,
Beautiful from the inside out.

Letting Go

The art of moving ourselves into the now.
Releasing the storms of past hurts.
Surrendering into the lessons of life.
Removing beliefs that keep us stuck in the darkness.
Softening our bodies and offering them love.
Taking down the masks of victimhood.
Dissolving the layers of fear.
Laying ourselves down in a field.
Looking up into the sapphire sky.
Floating away on a cloud.
Coming back to the earth.
Coming back to our hearts.
Letting go.
Breathing in.
Again, and again.

“I wonder how many people I’ve looked at all my life and never seen.”

-John Steinbeck

Invitation

I unroll my mat.
I allow the soft wanderings of my mind to empty.
I firmly plant my feet on the earth.
Grounding down into the ancient rhythms.
I feel the chattering of life.
I silence it with my breath.
My body becomes alive with sensation.
Invitation upon invitation.
Embodying Shakti
Receiving grace.
This practice delivers me from the suffering.
It invites me home.
I wander back to the inner landscape.
Here is the truest invitation.
Sit in the jewel of my heart and
live from this creative force.
I bow in honor.
Life invites me to practice once again.

Gratitude

Grateful for . . .

Eyes that behold.

Hands that create.

A tribe that supports.

Love that inspires.

Sunshine that warms.

Rains that cleanse.

Life that keeps offering its magic.

"Let no one ever come
to you without leaving
better and happier.
Be the living expression
of God's kindness;
kindness in your face,
kindness in your eyes,
kindness in your smile."

-Mother Teresa

I See You

I see you.
I feel the avalanche of conditioning.
Holding you hostage in the center of your being.
Breathe.
I see you.
Grasping for the familiar.
Holding on to the bricks of past foundations.
Breathe.
I see you.
Reaching for a higher way of being.
Surrendering to the discomfort of your growth.
Breathe.
I see you.
Becoming the artist of your life.
Becoming the author of your soul.
Breathe.
I see you.
Unfolding into the shape of your life.

"Until you make the
unconscious conscious,
it will direct your life
and you will call it fate."

-Carl Jung

Empowered

Stand with your feet firmly
rooted to the earth.
Pulsations of life trembling
beneath the surface.
You are a part of this life force.
Claim your right to be here.
Empowered by each
breath you take.
Enlivened by the movements
of your life.
See each choreographed
moment as an invitation to
begin again.
Reauthor.
Eliminate.
Renew.
You are not the stories
you tell yourself.
Do not become outraged by
these tales.
Begin a new story from a
stance of power.
How have you grown?
What have you learned?
Step into these questions
so that you can glean the
encouragement you need
to grow.
Empowerment is about growth.
Let it be uncomfortable.
Allow it to be messy.
But at the end of the day, do
not be outraged by life.
Feel that you are empowered.

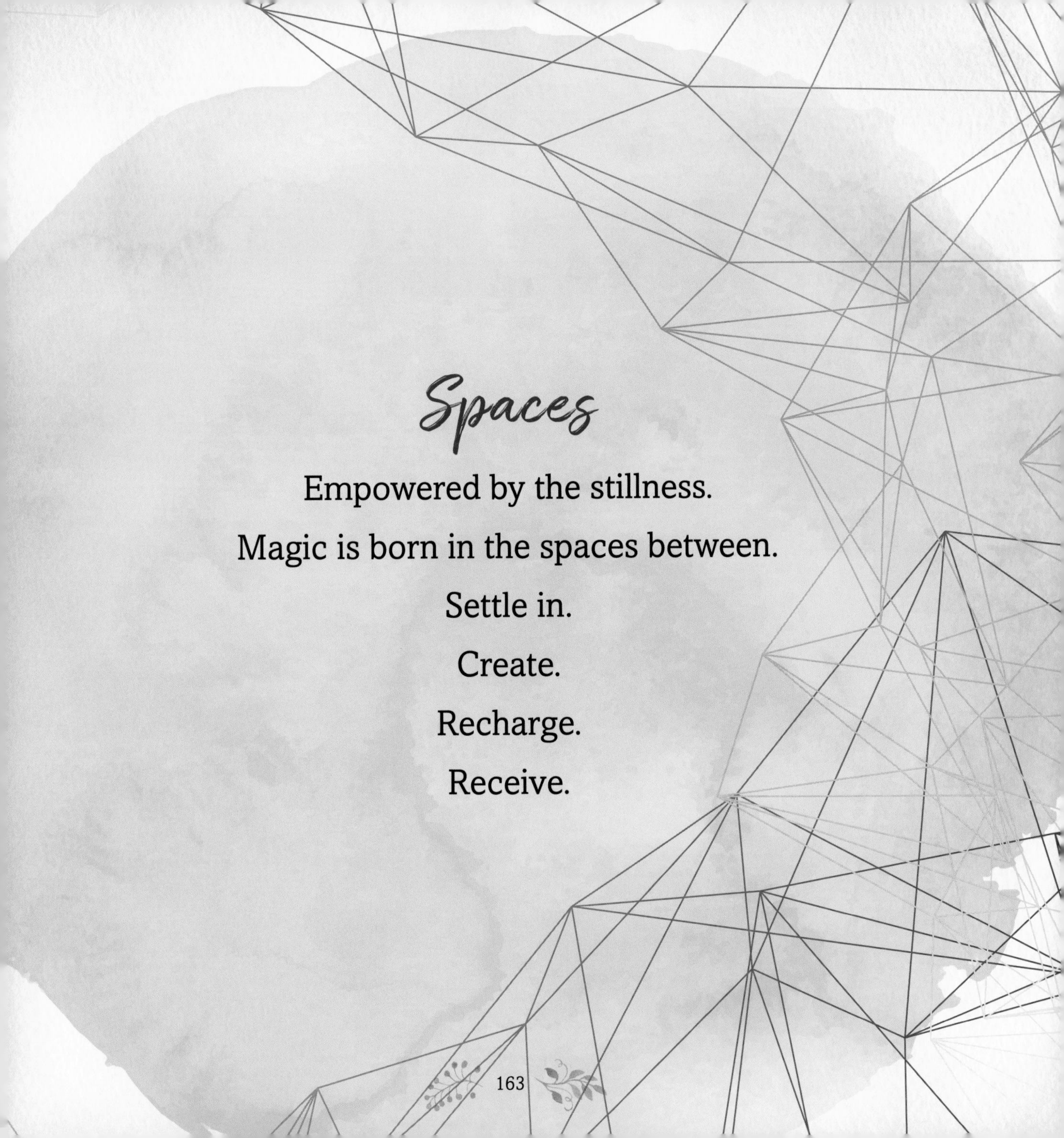

Spaces

Empowered by the stillness.

Magic is born in the spaces between.

Settle in.

Create.

Recharge.

Receive.

Freedom of Movement

Liberate yourself.
Expect the unexpected.
Feel the shower of blessings on their way.
Be in alignment with the wildness of your being.
Honor the ebb and flow.
Invite the genius of your knowing.
Allow confusion to fall to the floor.
Step into your brilliance.
Fly like a bird.
Soar like an eagle.
Dance like a goddess.
Rule like a queen.
Love like a king.
Cultivate a relationship to your freedom.
Own it.
Live it.
Embody it.
Take off.

"Not until we are lost do we begin to understand ourselves."

-Henry David Thoreau

Awake

Throw open your windows.
Unlock your doors.
Crawl out of your bed.
Free your mind.
Let in the winds of change.
Dance to a new day.
Free yourself of encumbered thoughts.
Shake loose the cords of others.
Value your ability to wake.
Unlearn all concepts of a substitute life.
This life.
Your life.
Priceless.
Awake.

Going Deep

Move past the surface of life.
Into the caverns of alchemy.
Step into your innate knowing.
Honor those who have gone before you.
You are mining for treasures below
the superficial ways of life.
These treasures are not always apparent.
Demand them like the trees demand leaves.
Like the sky demands the sun.
Move past the caution tape of your heart.
Maneuvering into the priceless landscape of your being.
Step on landmines of compassion.
Detonate kindness.
Travel toward your benevolent center.
Touch your sensitivities.
Understand your hurts.
Fan your tenderness.
Focus on your courage.
If you aren't willing to go deep,
Then who will?

“Beautiful people
do not just happen.”

-Elisabeth Kübler-Ross

Vulnerability

Become vulnerable like nature.
Offering yourself for a greater way of being.
Take off the seasons of masks.
The years of sinking into the quicksand
of others' desires for you.
Test your wings.
Invite what you admire.
Advocate for your heart.
Dissolve into the truth of this moment.
Tend to the ravenous nature of your being.
Get lost in the lusciousness of love.
Enter as a wise individual,
Connected to it all.
Allow the substance of this vulnerability to soothe you.
Drop in deeper.
Release blame.
Unhinge yourself from the burden of misfortune.
Arrange your heart in humbleness.
Become a victor of your vulnerability.
Time and time again.

“Everything changes once we identify with being the witness to the story, instead of the actor in it.”

-Ram Dass

Love

Commit to this energy.
Let go.
Free fall into the embrace of love.
Cease wrestling with your inhibitions.
Love is devoted to you.
Can you devote your life to love?
The fondness of this intimate companion.
Calling your name.
Delighting in your every move.
Desiring to know you in more inherent ways.
Claim your partnership with love.
Keep opening the door when this visitor appears.
Let yourself be touched.
Allow yourself to be devoured.
Create the environment for love to flourish.
Each day you must nourish the delicate energy.
Pause.
Breathe.
Offer yourself up.

Friendship

There is a tender field of acceptance within.
Frolic in this field.
Visit the earth again and again.
Come home to yourself.
There is no need to run.
Woman. Man.
Lover.
Daughter. Son.
Dreamer.
Beloved.
Welcome.
Befriend this moment.
Reach out in joy to all who dwell in this place.
Savor the intimate companions of life.

Advocate

For Mother Earth.
For Father Sky.
For broken hearts.
For grieving souls.
For gracious smiles.
For passionate causes.
For wonder-filled babes.
For astonished ways of living.
For innovative designs.
For out-of-the-box thinking.
For joy.
For passion.
For evolved approaches of thriving.
For fierceness.
Loving.
Living.
Relating.
Advocating.

“So, do it. Decide. Is this the life you want to life? Is this the person you want to love? Is this the best you can be? Ca you be stronger? Kinder? More compassionate? Decide. Breathe in. Breathe out and decide.”

-Grey's Anatomy TV show

Yield

Pause.
Have you yet considered the care within this moment?
All your floundering avoided.
Settle into the spaces between.
Yield.
Feel.
Perhaps that which you have been dazzled by is not meant for you.
Can you abandon these desires?
Allowing them to drop from you.
To melt like the polished glistening snow.
Yield.
Feel.
Life is delighted to offer you all that helps your soul to grow.
Eager to liberate you.
Feel.
Yield.
Surrender.

Transform

Deep within, there is a hearth of transformation.
A space where the kindling of love has been lit.
Passion for this breath.
And then the next.
An acceptance of living one's dharma.
See yourself transforming in the ashes.
Recollections of who you've been.
Embers of your life crackling at your feet.
Blazing through the layers of self.
Reflect as the flames devour your forgetfulness.
You have been forgetting for so long,
whom you truly are.
Become.
Emerge.
Transform.
Again and again.

New Beginnings

Go outside and take a deep breath.
Allow Mother Nature to shower you
with a sense of freedom.
This moment holds the chance to begin again.
See the beauty of changing form.
Of allowing loving awareness to encourage you.
Value that you are at a genius spot of intentionality.
Radiating possibilities.
Growing past the edges of comfort.
Committed to the solidness of your faith.
Do you even know how much this
new beginning desires you?
Craves to set you free?
Wants to create with you?
Wants to serenade you?

“People generally
see what they look for,
and hear what
they listen for.”

-Harper Lee

Birth

Practice each day earnestly giving birth.
Surrender to the discomfort.
Breathe.
Slow and gentle.
Soft and deep.
Moan with the trembling of your body.
Lean into the sensations.
Flow into the openings.
Welcome yourself.
Allow each contraction to propel you further toward your longing.
Life is emerging through you.
Whether you are creating a new project.
Birthing a babe.
Setting sail for new shores.
Feel the process delivering you toward a greater way of being.
Maturing you toward the impermeable nature of life.
Bow to yourself.
To the process of living.
Witness yourself.
Be with the sensitivities.
Melt.
Dissolve.
Be willing to give
birth each day.
You are forever
unfolding my love.

"Tell me, what is it you plan to do with your one wild and precious life?"

-Mary Oliver

Be With

Be with the edges.
Be with the straight lines.
Be with the tangles of life, as they wrap you up.
Be with the emotions, as they cascade over you.
Be with the fear.
Cradle it like you would a small child.
Offer compassion to this part of you who shrinks from life.
Be with the love.
The wild fields of possibilities.
The tender embrace of your lover.
Be with the joy.
The kind that wells up like a satisfied sea.
And spills into every corner of your life.
Be with the heartache.
Bow to this divine teacher.
This teacher who asks you to be more than you already are.
Be with the anger.
Allow it to transform you, as you slid underneath it.
Let the heat of this emotion transmute your old
ways of being.
Be with the uncertainty.
Trusting that each moment unfolds according to the timing of your life.
Welcome.
Soar into the winds and rise above like the eagle.
Be with all of it.
Attune yourself to the radiance of your foundation.

Shimmering

Settle into the harmony of being fully present.
Ground yourself into the wellspring of joy.
Witness your passions.
Participate in birthing them to life.
Dedicate your essence to creatively serving the light.
Gather up the brilliance of your power.
Share your unique, luminous light with the world.
Pause at your heart.
Can you feel your propensity to emanate pure love?
The kind that asks nothing in return.
Speak your truth clearly.
Allow your voice to be a healing balm.
Seek to know the unseen world
Trusting that you are a divine part of it all.
See so clearly.
Connect to the glow of all that is.
Breathe in from root to crown.
Circulate the light of your life.
Share your shimmering heart with the world.

“Live in the sunshine,
swim the sea,
Drink the wild air’s
salubrity.”

-Ralph Waldo Emerson

Hello Heart

I touch this tender memory keeper,
Nourishing the cracks.
Filling the fractures with light.
Honoring the spaces between the beats.
Each pitter patter records a moment of life.
I breathe in a sense of renewed openness.
Spaciousness.
Tenderness.
Hello, my dear heart.
How are you today?
Placing my hand on this beating vessel,
I trust that each moment contains an invitation.
Come in, beloved.
Live into the sensations of my life.

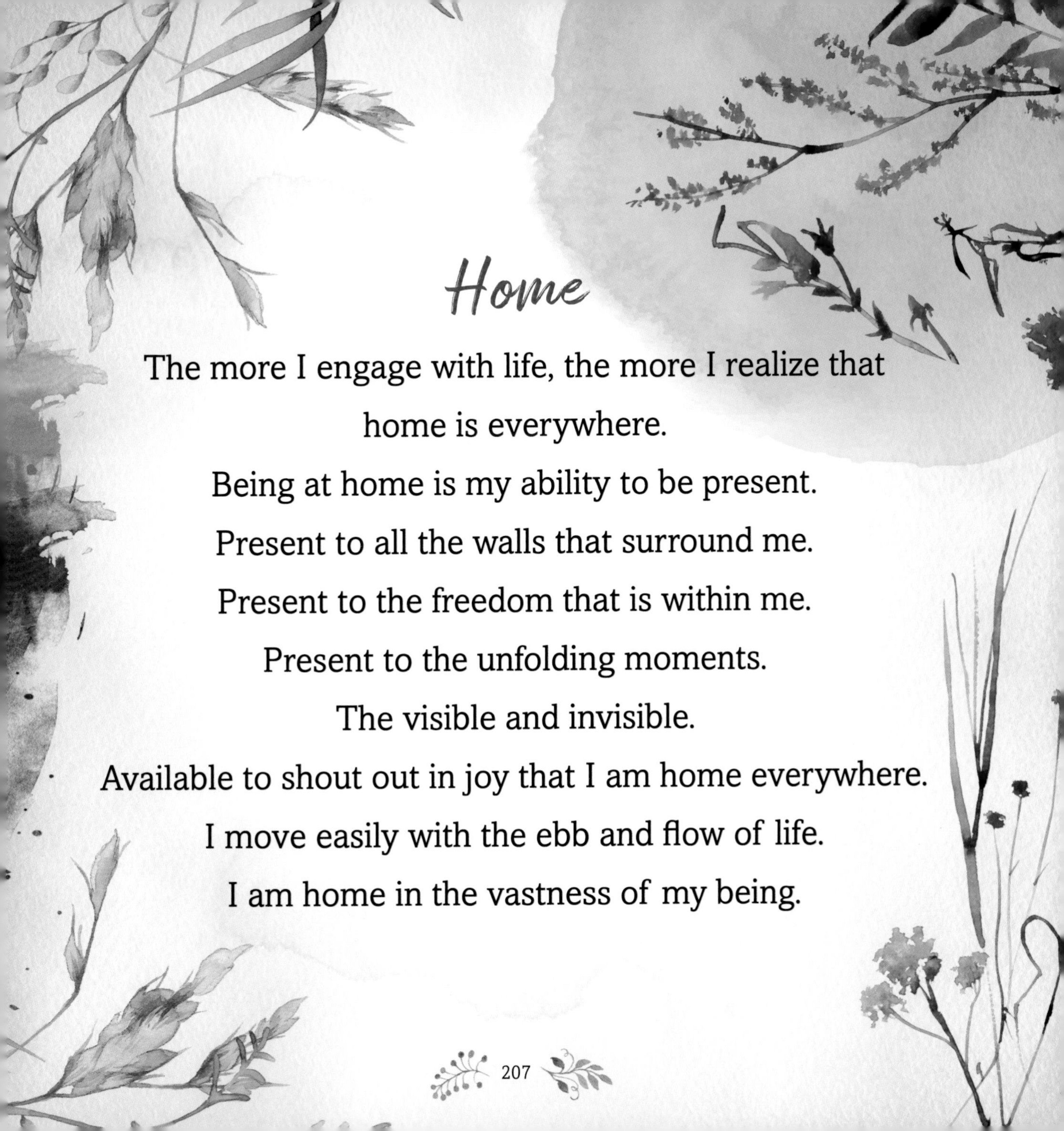

Home

The more I engage with life, the more I realize that
home is everywhere.
Being at home is my ability to be present.
Present to all the walls that surround me.
Present to the freedom that is within me.
Present to the unfolding moments.
The visible and invisible.
Available to shout out in joy that I am home everywhere.
I move easily with the ebb and flow of life.
I am home in the vastness of my being.

Seeking

I'm fairly sure we were born
with a certain sense
of curiosity.
The kind that wakes you at
night and makes
you stumble around
the familiar.
The act of seeking isn't
for the faint of heart.
It sometimes rips you from
the comforts of your life
and propels you into the
unknown.
It initiates a quest that calls
you to be an
explorer in uncharted lands.
To dive deep within the well
of your heart
to find the hidden treasures.
It asks you to announce your
place in the world.
To confidently assert
yourself in the hustle and
bustle of living.
To firmly stand with both
feet planted.
To breathe in the
magnificence of life.
Seeking will ask all of you.
To show up day after day.
Year after year.
Seeking will dazzle your
sight, if only you allow it.
May you always
sweetly seek.

Older

Smiling back are many familiar creases.

Lines of life strewn in zigs and zags.

Eyes that are attentive to the rich landscapes of life.

Delicate and tender.

Rich and wise.

Sacred moments flood like a rushing river.

This life is a grand puzzle of seeking.

Staring back at me, eyes filled with conviction.

All is as it should be,

The upsets gave way to grace.

The grief watered the seeds of newness.

The grand adventures cracked open my heart.

All the while, love held it all together.

I touch my hand to my face, and I realize
I've been both weathered and simultaneously made
more beautiful by life.
Transparency beckons me to see beneath the surface.
Beneath the stories of days gone by.
Yes, I am older, but perhaps this timetable has allowed
me to discover my true magic.
To embrace the mysteries of life.
And to still have the courage to say, "Life, I adore you."

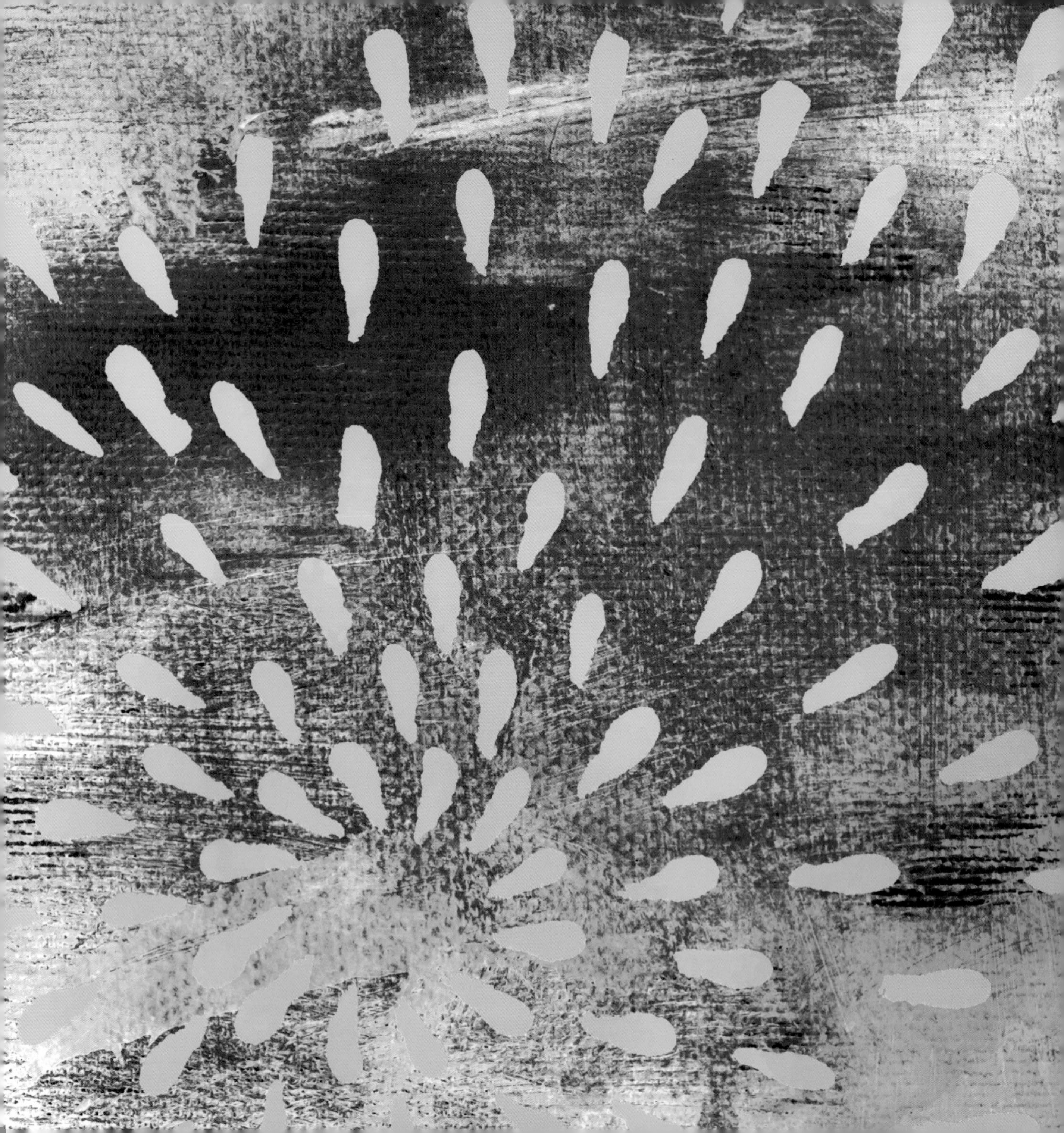

"Love, the poet said, is woman's whole existence."
-Virginia Woolf

ACKNOWLEDGMENTS

Sweetly Seeking was brought to life by many inspired hearts.

I would like to thank my book Sherpa and friend, Gail Kearns of To Press and Beyond, for her impeccable guidance and expertise throughout the creation of my second book. You continue to be a treasure in my life.

Lorraine Aillery, a beautiful philosopher and friend from Boulder, Colorado, has granted me great insights and invaluable opportunities to grow in the realm of my spiritual garden. Thank you for your thoughtful words so sweetly crafted to inspire readers to consider the landscapes of their hearts.

Alan and Ian of theBookDesigners, your design talents strike yet again. Thank you for your incredible visioning as you brought together another work of my heart.

Eleanor Williamson of Be Boulder Photography, thank you for capturing my love of life amid the Colorado sky. Your kindness and creativity are off the charts.

Mary Catherine Starr of Starr Struck, thank you for every hour of time, energy, and talent you poured into editing photos and creating the initial Sweetly Seeking logo. It is always a joy working with you.

To Kathy Moran, of Web Development Artistry, thank you for the phenomenal website and timely assistance as Cool Creative Press continues to grow.

To my family, thank you for your infinite love and support throughout my life. I adore each one of you!

To my tribe of friends, near and far, your presence in my life is priceless. Thank you for your love.

To all my teachers who have held a space of deep compassion for me to do my personal work, my heart is eternally grateful to you.

To the loving, benevolent source of all that is, thank you for this gift of life. I bow to you in profound love and amazement. Cheers to all the goodness that lies ahead. Aho!

I have been blessed by such an amazing community of hearts . . . to you all, thank you for sharing your divine light with me.

And to everyone reading this, thank you for diving into your life with courage and curiosity. May you sweetly seek all the days of your life.

ABOUT SARAH DICKEY

Sarah Dickey is a lover of life. Her enhancement with words began at a young age, and she has continued to cultivate this devotion into adulthood. Throughout her life, Sarah has passionately pursued various paths of personal growth and professional development. She is a certified transpersonal life coach, a yoga instructor, and an advanced heart-centered hypnotherapist.

As a visionary of change and a warrior of new philosophies, Sarah's enthusiasm to inspire is contagious. She believes we all have the capacity to author our own unique journeys and live revolutionary lives.

Sarah holds a bachelor of arts degree from Youngstown State University in Youngstown, Ohio, and a master's degree in education with an emphasis in clinical counseling from Malone University in Canton, Ohio. Sarah currently resides in the Northeast.

She is the author of *Ode to Love: A Journey of Awakening*. *Sweetly Seeking: Living an Inspired Life* is Sarah's second book.

ABOUT LORRAINE AILLERY BA, PHILOSOPHY

"A passionate life is a work of art to be created and expressed by each one of us." This credo, fulfilled through Lorraine's professional roles, both former and current, as a philosopher, an astrologer, a hypnotherapist, a mountaineer, a rock climber, and orator, and a gardener, has guided her to craft the life that she imagined as attainable. How she understands the world would not be possible without the parables that she encountered in the wilderness.

"What did I see today?" is what she asks when living the question.

A SPECIAL NOTE FROM THE AUTHOR AND FOUNDER OF COOL CREATIVE PRESS

It is my hope that this book becomes a treasure for you throughout your journey. It was an absolute delight bringing it to life. If you have enjoyed this book, I would greatly appreciate a short review on Amazon or your favorite book website. As an author, reviews are crucial to our success, so even a line or two can make a marked difference.

Also, please consider signing up for the Cool Creative Press (CCP) newsletter so that you can receive regular doses of inspiration and updates about CCP's emergence in the publishing world.
Visit www.coolcreativepress.com

As always, I welcome any comments or questions you might have and can be reached at sarah@coolcreativepress.com

REFERENCES

Page 13: Elizabeth Gilbert. *Big Magic: Creative Living beyond Fear* (Riverhead Books, 2016), 8.

Page 19: Virginia Woolf. *Moments of Being* (Harcourt Brace & Company, 1976).

Page 24: Rumi. As quoted in "Death: The Teacher of Life?" *Huffpost* (January 4, 2015).

Page 31: Albert Einstein. As quoted in the *Journal of France and Germany* by Gilbert Fowler White in *Living with Nature's Extremes: The Life of Gilbert Fowler White* (Johnson Books, 2006), 62.

Page 36: Bhagavad Gita, chapter 3, verse 35.

Page 43: Anaïs Nin. *Seduction of the Minotaur* (The Swallow Press, 1961), 124.

Page 48: Viktor E. Frankl. *Man's Search for Meaning* (Pocket Books, 1997), 135.

Page 55: Joseph Campbell. *A Joseph Campbell Companion: Reflections on the Art of Living* (Joseph Campbell Foundation, 2011), 15.

Page 60: Oscar Wilde. "The Soul of Man under Socialism," *Fortnightly Review* (February 1891), 292.

Page 69: Wayne W. Dyer. *The Essential Wayne Dyer Collection* (Hay House, 2013).

Page 74: Vincent van Gogh. Letter dated September 18, 1888, written in French by Vincent van Gogh to his brother Theo. Van Gogh Museum, Amsterdam. Translation into English by Van Gogh Letters Project.

Page 79: Erin Hanson. *thepoeticunderground* (lulu.com, 2016), 9.

Page 90: George Bernard Shaw. *George Bernard Shaw: An Unsocial Life* (A Word to the Wise, 2015).

Page 95: Hafiz. *The Gift* (Penguin Compass, 1999), 228.

Page 100: Robert Frost. As quoted in "Robert Frost's Secret" by Ray Josephs in *This Week Magazine* (September 1954).

Page 109: Roald Dahl. *The Minpins* (Puffin Books, 2009), 48.

Page 114: Psalm 46:10. Holy Bible (New International Version, 2011).

Page 119: Swami Vivekananda. *The Complete Works of Swami Vivekananda* (Advaita Ashrama, 1947).

Page 124: Henry David Thoreau. *The Journal, 1837-1861* (NYRB Classics, 2009), 598.

Page 132: Ram Dass. *Walking Each Other Home* (Sounds True, 2018).

Page 139: Sharon Salzberg. *Lovingkindness: The Revolutionary Art of Happiness* (Boston, 2008), 123.

Page 142: Zora Neale Hurston. *Their Eyes Were Watching God* (Harper, 2000), 25.

Page 149: John Steinbeck. *The Winter of Our Discontent* (The Viking Press, 1961), chapter 4.

Page 155: Mother Teresa. As quoted in *A Pocketful of Promises* (Honor Books, 2004), 157.

Page 158: Carl Jung. *Visions: Notes of the Seminar Given in 1930–1934 by C. G. Jung* (Princeton University Press, 1997).

Page 167: Henry David Thoreau. *Thoreau and the Art of Life: Reflections on Nature and the Mystery of Existence* (North Atlantic Books, 2010), 79.

Page 172: Elisabeth Kübler-Ross. *Death: The Final Stage of Growth* (Scribner, 1975), 93.

Page 177: Ram Dass. "The Wisdom of Ram Dass," *The Responsive Universe* (November 17, 2016).

Page 184: *Grey's Anatomy.* "Seal Our Fate" [10.1]. Richard Webber (played by James Pickens) speaking in a voiceover.

Page 193: Harper Lee. *To Kill a Mockingbird* (Harper, 2002), 198.

Page 196: Mary Oliver. "The Summer Day," as quoted in *Saved by a Poem* by Kim Rosen (Hay House, 2009), 142.

Page 203: Ralph Waldo Emerson. "Merlin's Song," *Poems* (Houghton, Mifflin and Company, 1904).

Page 215: Virginia Woolf. *Orlando: A Biography* (Marine Books, 1973), 268.

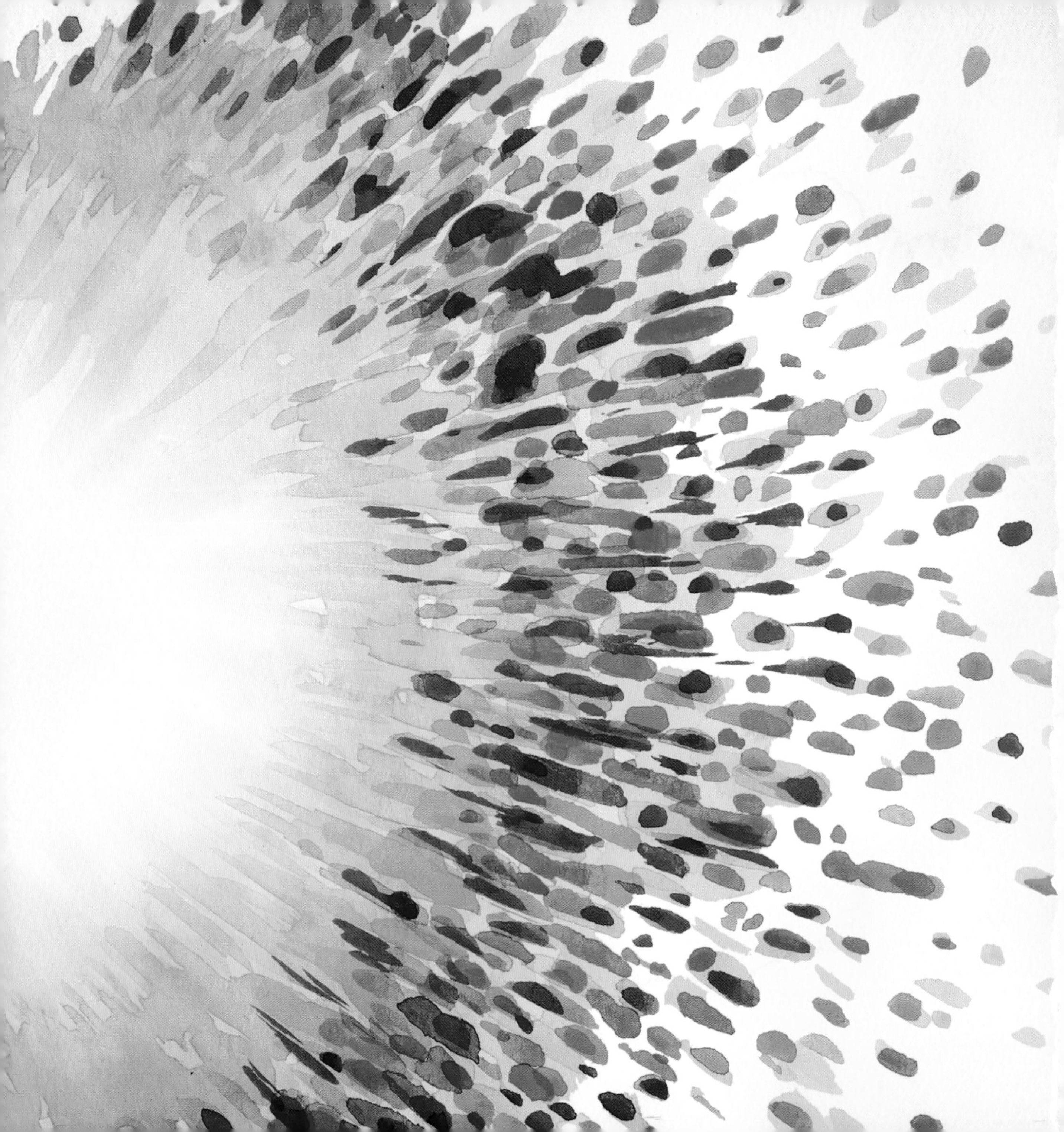